Science Olympiad

Class 02

A must have book for all
Olympiads & Talent Search Exams...

by
Akriti Verma

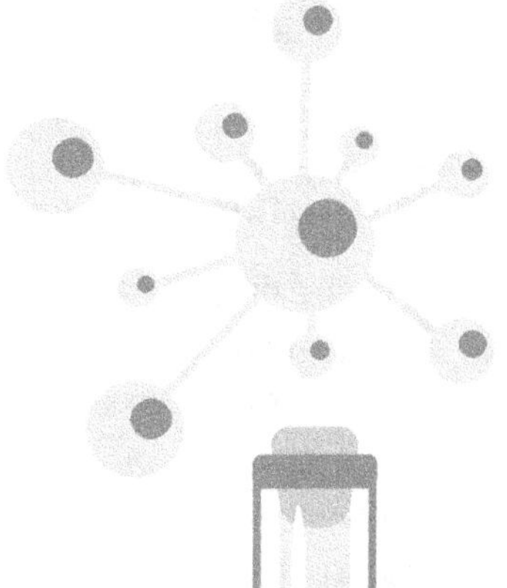

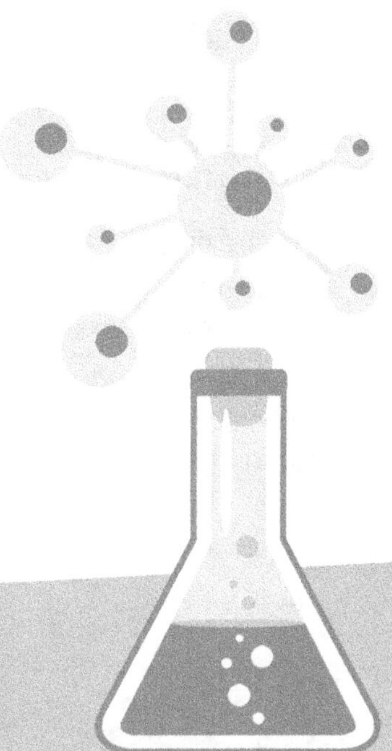

BLOOM CAP
Bloom Cap Edu Ventures Pvt. Ltd.

BLOOM CAP
Bloom Cap Edu Ventures Pvt. Ltd.

Administrative & Production Office
'Ramchhaya' 4577/15, Agarwal Road, Darya Ganj, New Delhi -110002
Tele: 011- 47630600, 43518550

ISBN: 978-93-25519-31-2

PRICE: ₹100.00

PO No: TXT-XX-XXXXXXX-X-XX

For further information about the books log on to
www.bloomcap.org

Follow us on

Preface

"Future belongs to those Who prepares for it today"

School Olympiads are National & International level competitions conducted by different Government, Non-Government & Educational Organisations with the purpose of making the children ready to face competitive exams.

The challenging Questions asked in Olympiads motivate them to learn more & more and bring out the best result with improved academic performance. The Awards & Scholarship offered by Olympiads motivate children to aspire & strive for doing better and emerge out to be the best.

Science Olympiads

Being a Scientist or Engineer or Doctor has always been a dream of each school going child. A good command over Science is a must for any of these. Questions of Science Olympiads are structured to help students to develop scientific temperament & motivate them to understand the concepts of science. They also focuses on improving existing knowledge of a student by adding more information.

'Bloom Science Olympiad Study Book Class 2' is a perfect resource to Study & Practice for Olympiad Exams and other National & State Level Talent Search Exams & Other Competitions.

Some Special Features of Bloom Science Olympiad Study Books are;

- Chapterwise Exercises having different types of Objective Questions; Analytical, Applications, Remembering etc, at par with the Olympiad Level.
- Detailed Explanation for each question.
- Olympiad Pattern Practice Sets at the end.

This book is prepared by Expert Panel with the utmost care, still if you have any suggestions regarding its improvement then feel free to contact us at olympiads@bloomcap.org. We will try to inculcate your suggestions in the further editions.

Contents

Chapter 01

Living and Non-living Things

- All things we see around us are either living or non-living things. Things which have life in them are called living things, e.g. Plants, animals and human beings.

Living things

- Living things can feel, move, grow and reproduce. They need air, water and food to grow and live.
- Things which do not have life in them are called non-living things, e.g. Plastic bottles, mountains, computer, etc. They are divided into two categories as :

Non-living Things

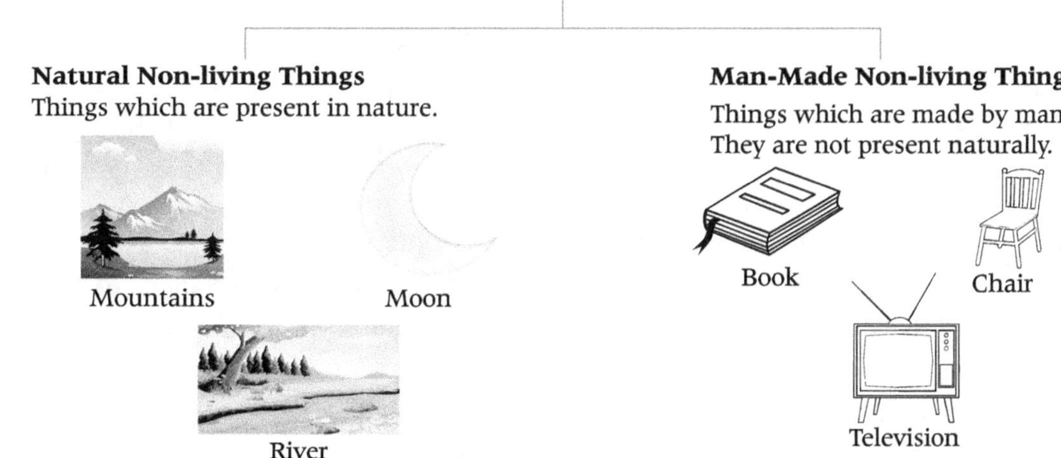

Natural Non-living Things
Things which are present in nature.

Mountains

Moon

River

Man-Made Non-living Things
Things which are made by man.
They are not present naturally.

Book

Chair

Television

- Non-living things cannot feel, move, grow and reproduce.

Let's Practice

1. Which of the following is a natural non-living thing?

(a)  (b) 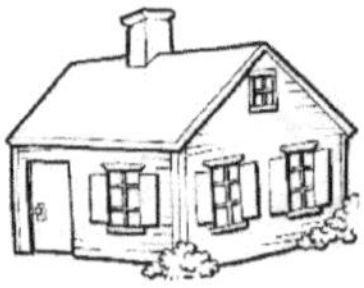 (c) 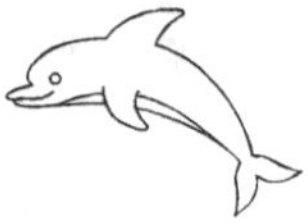 (d) 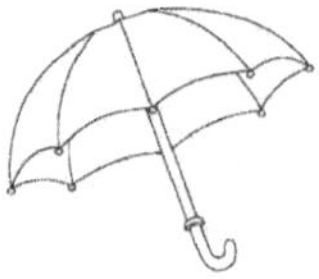

2. Read the following table. Which of the following thing is wrongly placed?

Living things	Non-living things
Dog	The Sun
Cat	TV
Computer	Chair

(a) Cat
(b) Computer
(c) Chair
(d) None of these

3. Which of the following is a living thing?

(a) 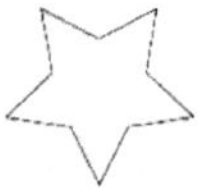 (b) (c)  (d) 

4. Non-living things can only be
(a) Natural (b) Man made (c) Both (a) and (b) (d) None of these

5. Which of the following living thing(s) cannot move from one place to another by itself?

(a)  (b)  (c)  (d) 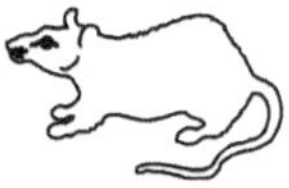

6. Write 'T' for true statement and 'F' for false statement.
I. A plant can grow.
II. Dogs can move from one place to another.
III. Aeroplane can fly on their own.

Codes

	I	II	III
(a)	T	T	F
(b)	F	T	F
(c)	T	F	T
(d)	F	F	T

7. Which of the following things cannot grow, become old and then die ?

(a)  (b)  (c)  (d) 

8. Which is not common about birds and plants?
   (a) Both are living things
   (b) Both can fly
   (c) Both can breathe
   (d) Both can grow

9. Which of the following differences are correct about the bird and aeroplane?

	Bird	Aeroplane
1.	Living thing	Non-living thing
2.	Cannot fly	Can fly
3.	Mostly seen in sky	Mostly seen on trees

   (a) Only 1
   (b) Only 2
   (c) Both (1) and (3)
   (d) All are correct

10. Why do animals move from one place to another?
   (a) To look for food (b) To look for water (c) To look for shelter (d) All of these

11. Living things need .... to grow .
   (a) water
   (b) clothes
   (c) food
   (d) Both (a) and (c)

12. When Rahul was walking in a garden he saw a 'touch me not plant' there. He touches that plant and noticed that the leaves of touch me not plant getting closed.

   What does conclusion can be made from above information about touch me not plant?
   (a) Touch me not plant is a poisonous plant
   (b) Touch me not plant response to touch
   (c) Touch me not plant get afraid
   (d) None of the above

13. Plants make their food from ....
   (a) sunlight
   (b) moonlight
   (c) starlight
   (d) flashlight

14. What would happen if living thing do not get air?
   (a) They would remain healthy
   (b) They grow fast
   (c) They would die
   (d) All of these

15. All living things feel changes around them. Plants grow towards the light. It shows that plant also ..*A*.. but plants do not have ..*B*..

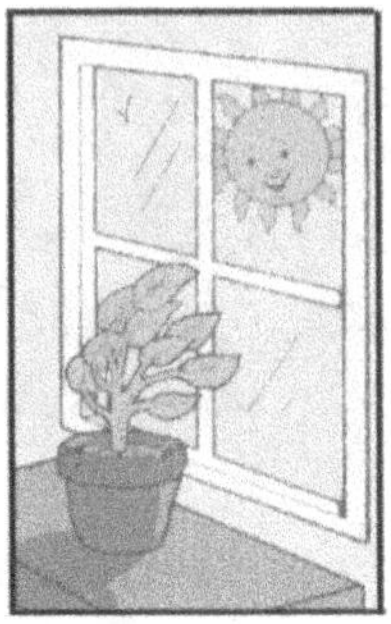

Plants grow towards light

(a) *A*– move, *B*– leaves
(b) *A*– bend, *B*–skin
(c) *A*– feel, *B*–sense organs
(d) *A*– move, *B*–root

16. Look at the picture carefully and choose the correct option.

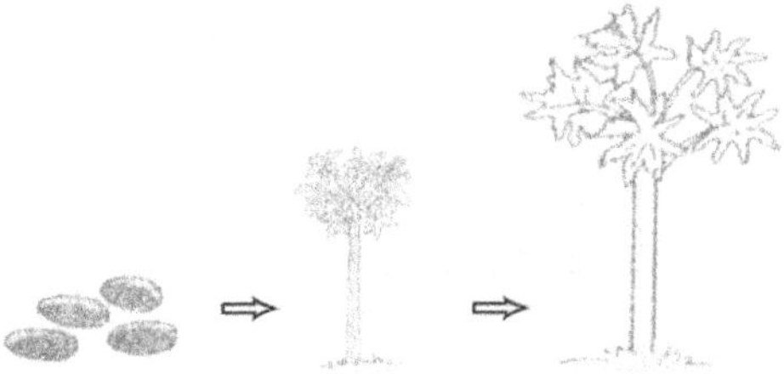

(Seed)

A seed is a living thing because
(a) it grows into a plant (b) it does not breathe (c) it does not move (d) it does not grow

17. We are surrounded by many living things and non-living things. So, classify them as living or non-living.

A.  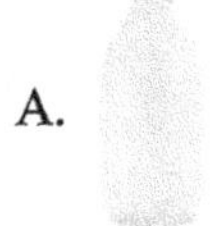
B. 
C. 
D. 

Codes

	A	B	C	D
(a)	Living	Non-living	Non-living	Living
(b)	Non-living	Living	Non-living	Non-living
(c)	Non-living	Living	Living	Non-living
(d)	Living	Non-living	Living	Non-living

18. Which one of the following refers to non-living things?

(a) Fan, kite, bird (b) Table, chair, child

(c) Clouds, rivers, mountains (d) Rivers, birds, trees

19. Which of the following non-living things cannot be moved by humans?

(a) Mountain (b) Teddy (c) Chair (d) Car

20. Ram kept a frog with some insects in a jar. After sometimes, he saw that the frog faints. He thinks what would happen to the frog as he left the food for the frog in the jar?

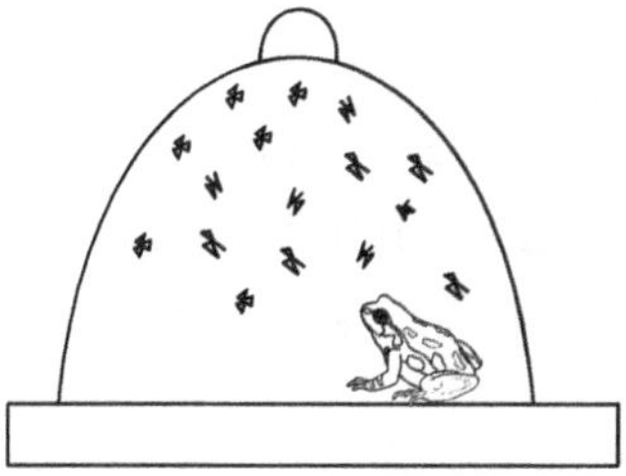

Which of the following thing frog needs to live?

(a) Food (b) Air (c) Light (d) Clothes

21. Solve the riddle

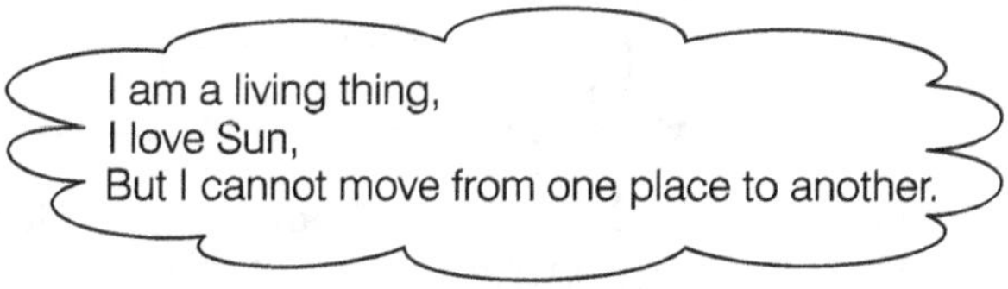

(a) Sunflower (b) Bird (c) Cat (d) Human

22. Study the given characteristics shown by Q and R

	Moves from place to place	Can breathe	Can grow	Has legs
Q	×	✓	✓	×
R	✓	✓	✓	✓

Identify Q and R.

	Q	R
(a)	Plants	Humans
(b)	Birds	Humans
(c)	Humans	Mountains
(d)	Computers	Rivers

Chapter
02

Plants

- Plants are most precious gift of nature. It helps to keep air fresh and clean.
- We get many useful things from plants like fruits, vegetables, spices, cereals, pulses, etc.
- There are different types of plants in our surrounding.

Parts of Plant

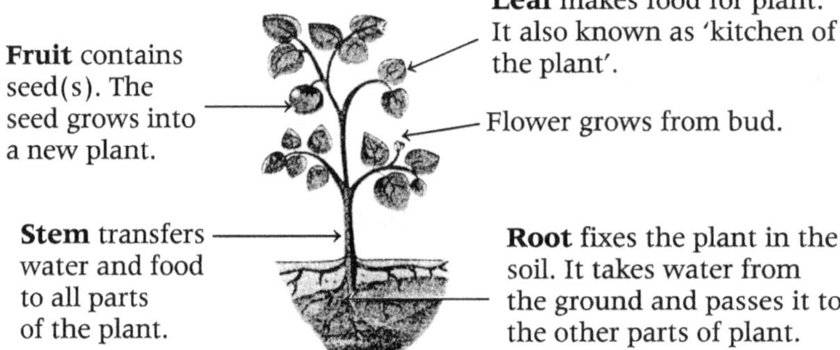

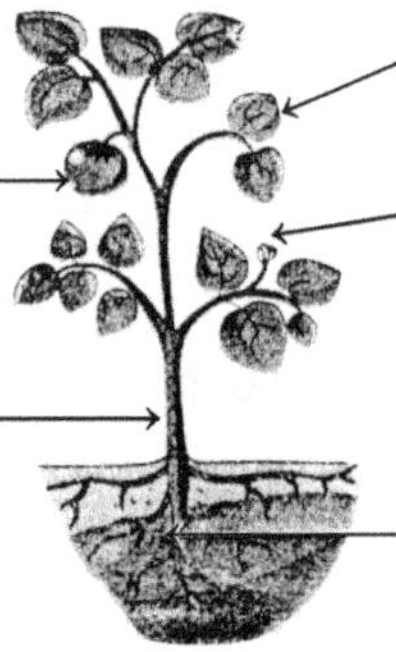

Different Types of Plants

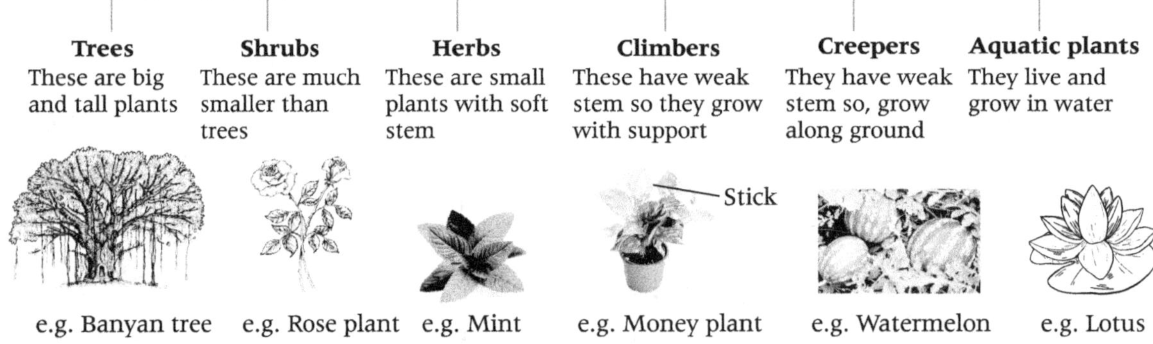

- **Trees**
  These are big and tall plants

  e.g. Banyan tree
- **Shrubs**
  These are much smaller than trees

  e.g. Rose plant
- **Herbs**
  These are small plants with soft stem

  e.g. Mint
- **Climbers**
  These have weak stem so they grow with support

  e.g. Money plant
- **Creepers**
  They have weak stem so, grow along ground

  e.g. Watermelon
- **Aquatic plants**
  They live and grow in water

  e.g. Lotus

Let's Practice

1. Which part of plant is known as the 'kitchen of plant'?
   (a) Roots (b) Leaves (c) Stem (d) Fruits

2. Match the following columns.

	Column I		Column II
A.	 Bamboos	1.	To make medicine
B.	 Tulsi	2.	To make sugar
C.	 Jasmine	3.	To make furniture
D.	 Sugarcane	4.	To make perfumes

Codes

	A	B	C	D		A	B	C	D
(a)	2	1	3	4	(b)	3	1	4	2
(c)	1	3	4	2	(d)	1	2	4	3

3. Which of the following is found in a desert?

(a)  (b)  (c)  (d) 

4. Which of the following plant is climber?

A

B

C

D

(a) Only *A* (b) Only *B* (c) Only *C* (d) Only *D*

5. Which part of the plant absorb water and minerals for the growth of plant?
(a) Leaves (b) Stem (c) Branches (d) Root

6. The leaves of a neem tree are used as

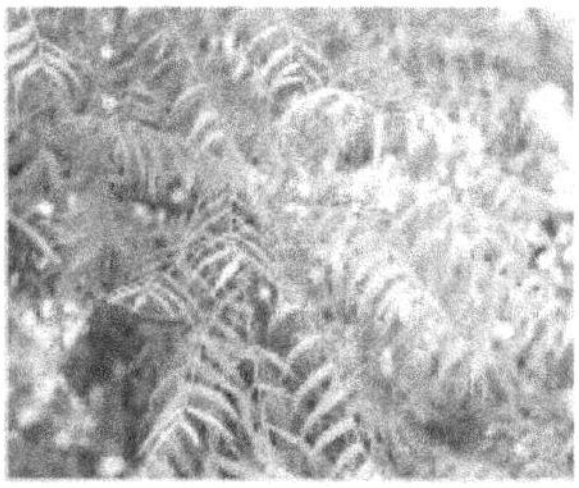

(a) spices (b) paper (c) medicine (d) rubber

7. Which of the following plant(s) is/are live only for one season?

Mint
A

Coriander
B

Tulsi
C

(a) Only *A* (b) Only *B* (c) Only *C* (d) All of these

8. Which natural fibre is obtained from this plant?

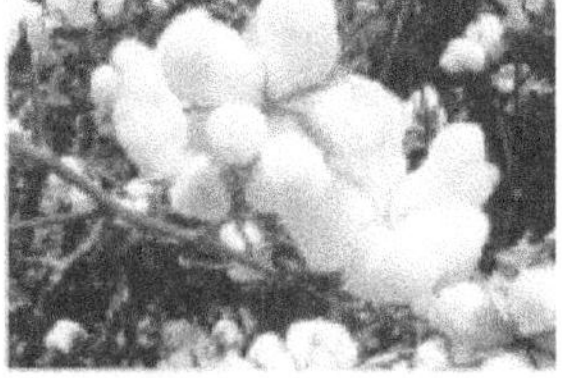

(a) Cotton (b) Jute (c) Wool (d) Leather

9. Match the following columns.

Column I		Column II
A.	 Lotus	1. Herb
B.	 Rose	2. Shrub
C.	 Mint	3. Water plant

Codes

	A	B	C		A	B	C
(a)	3	2	1	(b)	1	2	3
(c)	1	3	2	(d)	2	3	1

10. Which of the plant is used to make chapati (roti)?

(a) 

(b) 

(c) 

(d) 

11. Which of the following statement is not correct?

(a) Herbs are very small plant

(b) Trees are smaller than shrubs

(c) Creepers grow along the ground

(d) Climbers need support to grow and stand

12. Which of the following are example of medicinal plants?

(a) Turmeric, neem (b) Neem, rose (c) Rose, lotus (d) *Cactus*, mango

13. Which of the following are example of aquatic plants?

(a) Lotus, water lily (b) Lotus, rose (c) Sunflower, rose (d) Rose, water lily

14. The following plants are examples of

Money plant

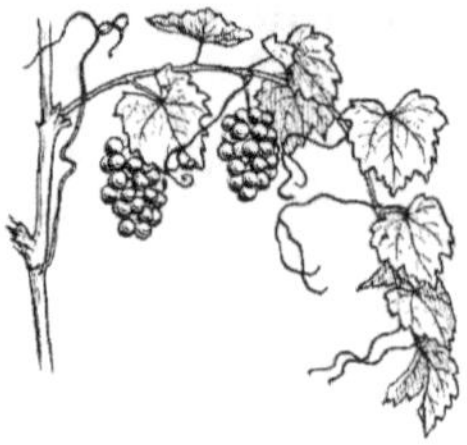

Grapevine

(a) creepers (b) climbers (c) shrubs (d) herbs

15. We get oil from which of these plants?

(a) 

(b) 

(c) 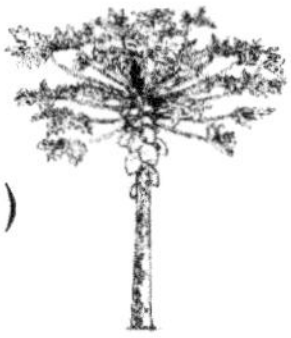

(d) 

16. Guess my name

I am a shrub,

Nehru chacha loves me,

You used my flower for making perfumes

Who am I?

(a) Rose (b) Marigold
(c) Cauliflower (d) Lotus

17. Cotton fibres are used for

(a) making perfumes (b) making clothes
(c) making ropes (d) making dishes

18. Which of the following is an edible flower?

(a) Rose (b) Cauliflower
(c) Lotus (d) Lily

19. From the following items, select the things which we get from plants.

Medicines, cereals, fibres, meat, fruits, vegetables, spices, leather

How many things are we get from plants?

(a) 6 (b) 5 (c) 3 (d) 8

20. Identify *X, Y* and *Z*.

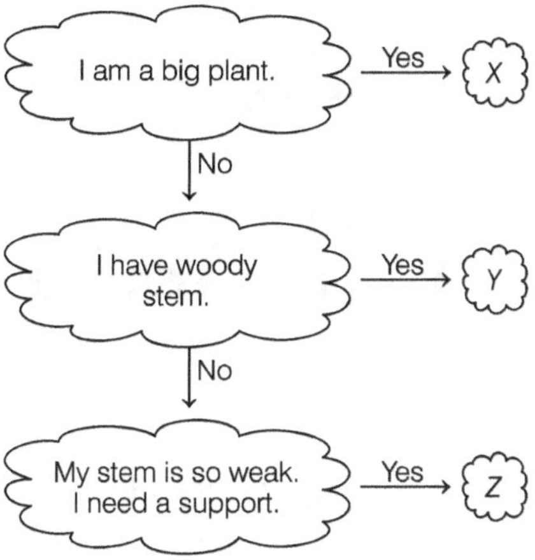

	X	*Y*	*Z*
(a)	Climber	Creeper	Herb
(b)	Tree	Herb	Shrub
(c)	Herb	Shrub	Climber
(d)	Tree	Shrub	Climber

21. Fill the correct options in the given blanks.

I. Plant grows from................ .
II. The fruit grows from the ....
III. Buds grow on the ....

Codes

	I	II	III
(a)	roots	seed	leaves
(b)	roots	seed	stem
(c)	seed	flower	stem
(d)	seed	leaves	branches

22. Which fruit is not grown on trees?

(a) 

(b) 

(c) 

(d) 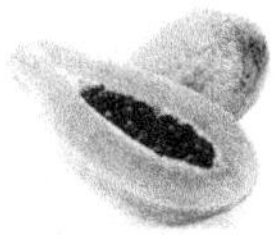

Chapter 03

Animals

Kinds of Animals

- Domestic animals (Live with us) e.g. Dog, cat, parrot.
- Farm animals (Live in farms) e.g. Goat, cow, hen.
- Wild animals (Live in forest) e.g. Lion, tiger, zebra.
- Aquatic animals (Live in water) e.g. Fish, dolphin.
- Birds (can fly and eat insects) e.g. Swan, penguin.
- Insects (has six legs and one or two pairs of wings).

Butterfly

Housefly

Ladybird

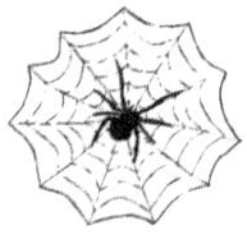
Spider

Animals and their Food

- **Herbivores** Some animals eat plants only. They are called as plant eating animals, e.g. Giraffe, cow, buffalo, goat, sheep, etc.
- **Carnivores** Some animals eat flesh of others animal only. They are called as flesh eating animals, e.g. Lion, tiger, snake, crocodile, eagle, etc.
- **Omnivores** Some animals eat both plants and flesh of other animals. They are called as both plant and flesh eating animals, e.g. Bear, dog, crow, fox, etc.

Animals and their Homes

Many animals lived in a different namely homes. Some homes are natural homes, like den, cave, burrow, etc. while some homes are man-made like kennel, shed, etc.

Different Things we get from Animals

- Wool giving animals are sheep, goat, rabbit, etc.
- Milk giving animals are goat, cow, buffalo, etc.
- Silk giving animals are silkworm, etc.
- Honey and wax giving animals are honeybees, etc.

Let's Practice

1. Which of the following animals give us milk?

(a)  (b)  (c)  (d) All of these

2. Domestic animals depend on humans for ....
(a) shelter (b) food and water (c) care (d) All of these

3. Which one of the following is not a plant eating animal?

(a)  (b)  (c)  (d) 

4. Match the animals with their food.

Column I	Column II
A. 	1. 
B. 	2. 
C. 	3. 
D. 	4. 

Codes

	A	B	C	D		A	B	C	D
(a)	2	3	4	1	(b)	3	4	2	1
(c)	3	2	1	4	(d)	2	4	3	1

5. ...... make honey from the juice of flowers.
(a) Butterfly (b) Silkworm (c) Mosquito (d) Honeybee

6. Look at the following figures *A* and *B*.

A

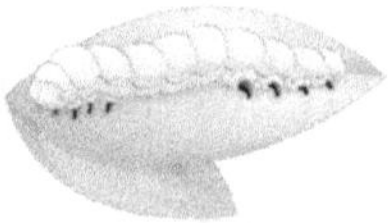

Silkworms

B

These animals provide us

(a) milk and egg

(b) fur and egg

(c) wool and silk thread

(d) milk and silk thread

7. Which one of the following animals does not carry loads?

(a) Bullock (b) Camel (c) Donkey (d) Dog

8. Match the animals with their homes.

	Column I		**Column II**
A.	 Cow	1.	 Shed
B.	 Horse	2.	 Den
C.	 Lion	3.	 Kennel
D.	 Dog	4.	 Stable

Codes

	A	B	C	D
(a)	1	4	2	3
(b)	2	3	1	4
(c)	4	1	3	2
(d)	3	2	4	1

9. Which animal is used to plough the field?
(a) Oxen (b) Horses (c) Donkeys (d) Elephants

10. Which of the following animal gives us both eggs and meat?
(a) Duck (b) Hen (c) Ostrich (d) Snakes

11. Bear is a...*A*... animal which eat ...*B*... of other animals. Here, *A* and *B* is

	A	*B*
(a)	Wild	Plant eating
(b)	Domestic	Flesh eating
(c)	Wild	Both plant and flesh
(d)	Domestic	Plant eating

12. Which option is not correct about the given animal?

(a) It lives in desert
(b) It is also called as ship of desert
(c) It eats flesh of other animals
(d) It is used for carrying loads

13. Identify *X* in the given flow chart.

Animals
- Plant eating: Giraffe, Elephant
- Flesh eating: Lion, Tiger
- Both plant and flesh eating: Bear, *X*

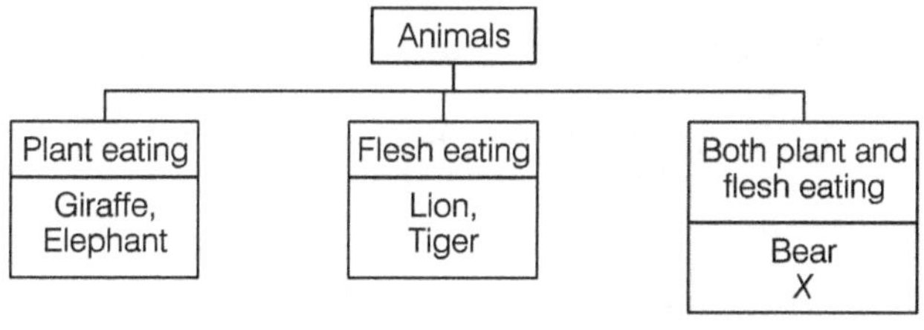

(a) Dog (b) Goat (c) Snake (d) Cow

14. I have four legs and a big and strong tail.
I am very dangerous.
I am the strongest animal in water.

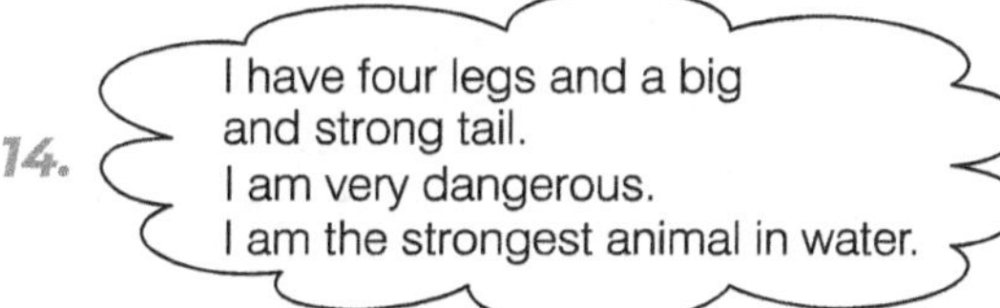

Who am I ?
(a) Giraffe
(b) Crocodile
(c) Ostrich
(d) Tiger

15. Which of the following animals gives us milk and meat?

(a)  Pig

(b)  Goat

(c)  Hen

(d)  Horse

16. Following items is made from the ...... of animals.

(a) teeth (b) wool (c) skin (d) dung

17. Which of the following group shows aquatic animals?

(a)  Snake  Frog

(b)  Whale  Tiger

(c)  Fish  Dolphin

(d)  Rabbit  Rhinoceros

18. Which of the among these are flightless bird?

(a) 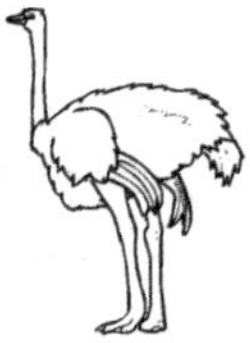 Ostrich

(b)  Kiwi

(c)  Penguin

(d) All of these

19. Solve the riddle.

I have six legs,
I have colourful wings,
I love flowers.

Who am I ?

(a) Butterfly (b) Spider (c) Mosquito (d) Honeybee

20. Match the following columns.

	Column I		Column II
A.	King of jungle	1.	Camel
B.	National bird	2.	Tiger
C.	National animal	3.	Lion
D.	Ship of desert	4.	Peacock

Codes

	A	B	C	D
(a)	3	4	1	2
(b)	3	4	2	1
(c)	4	1	3	2
(d)	1	2	3	4

21. Identify *P* and *Q*.

I. *P* lives in forest, but not eat plants.

II. *Q* not live in forest, but eat plants.

Choose the correct option.

(a) *P* - Tiger, *Q* - Zebra
(b) *P* - Elephant, *Q* - Crocodile
(c) *P* - Lion, *Q* - Zebra
(d) *P* - Lion, *Q* - Goat

Chapter 04

Human Body

- Human body is made up of bones, muscles and different organs.
- There are 206 bones in human body. When all bones are arranged in proper way, they form a skeleton.
- Parts of body that we can see are called **external organs**. These organs help us to understand and know things around us and are called as **sense organs**.
- Organs which are inside our body and we cannot see them are called **internal organs**.
- Some organs are called as sense organs. Sense organs help us to understand and to know things around us.
- Some other organs are important to maintain our body health.

External/Sense Organs

Human body have five sense organs as follows

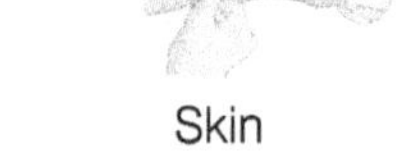

Sense Organs	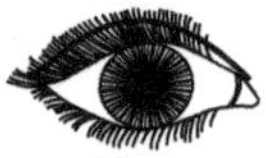 Eye	 Ears	 Tongue	 Nose	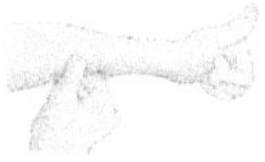 Skin
Functions	It helps us to see	It helps us to hear	It helps us to taste	• It helps us to smell. • It also helps in breathing	• It covers the entire body. • It helps us to feel. • It is the largest sense organ

Internal Organs

Organs	Functions
Heart	It helps us to pump our blood throughout the body.
Lungs	It helps us in breathing.
Stomach	It helps us in digestion. It is also known as store house of food as it contains food for long hours.
Brain	It is placed inside our skull. It controls our body actions like thinking, learning, etc.
Kidneys	It helps us to remove waste materials from our body.

Let's Practice

1. How many sense organs are present in our body?
   (a) 3　(b) 2　(c) 1　(d) 5
2. Our body is made up of …… .
   (a) muscles　(b) bones　(c) organs　(d) All of these
3. Which of the following organ is used in breathing?
   (a) 
   Large intestine
   (b) 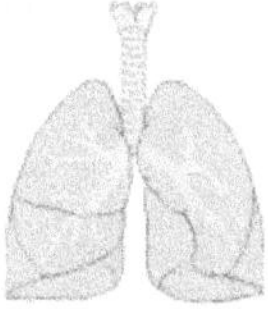
   Lungs
   (c) 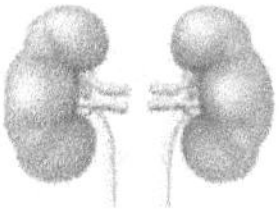
   Kidney
   (d) 
   Heart
4. Which of the following organ control all our actions like seeing, hearing, walking and learning?
   (a) 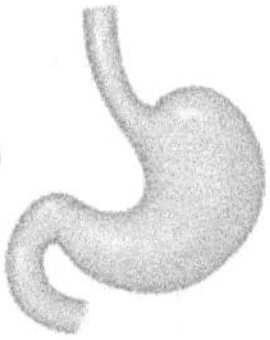
   Stomach
   (b) 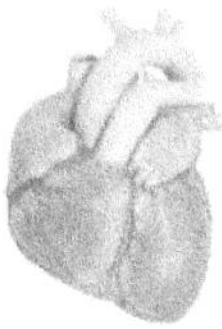
   Heart
   (c) 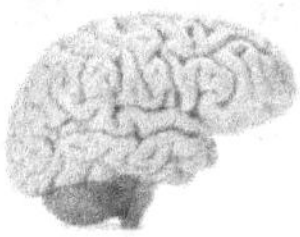
   Brain
   (d) All of these
5. Ramu while preparing tea got a burn. Which sense organ help him to sense the hotness?
   (a) Eyes　(b) Ears　(c) Skin　(d) Both (a) and (c)
6. Match the sense organs with their function.

Column I	Column II
A. 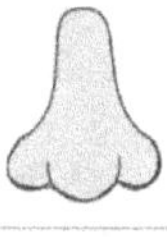	1. 
B. 	2. 
C. 	3. 
D. 	4. 

Codes

	A	B	C	D		A	B	C	D
(a)	4	3	1	2	(b)	1	2	3	4
(c)	3	4	2	1	(d)	3	4	1	2

7. How many bones are there in our body?
(a) 200 bones (b) 210 bones (c) 206 bones (d) 306 bones

8. Which is the largest sense organ in our body?
(a) Eyes (b) Ears (c) Skin (d) Nose

9. Which part is incorrectly matched?

	Function	Organ
(a)	Pumping of blood	Heart
(b)	Breathing	Ribs
(c)	Digestion of food	Stomach
(d)	Thinking process	Brain

10. The given figure shows a black box containing an object. Kunal put his hand into the box and made the following comments.

It is cold.
It is rough.
It is hard.

Which sense organ is involved to make these descriptions?
(a) Ear (b) Tongue (c) Skin (d) Nose

11. Write 'T' for true statement and 'F' for false statement.
I. We have four sense organs.
II. We see with our ears.
III. We feel things with our skin.

Codes

	I	II	II		I	II	II
(a)	T	T	T	(b)	T	F	F
(c)	T	F	T	(d)	F	F	T

12. Solve the given riddle.

I am the sense organ,
I have no bones,
I helps you to taste.

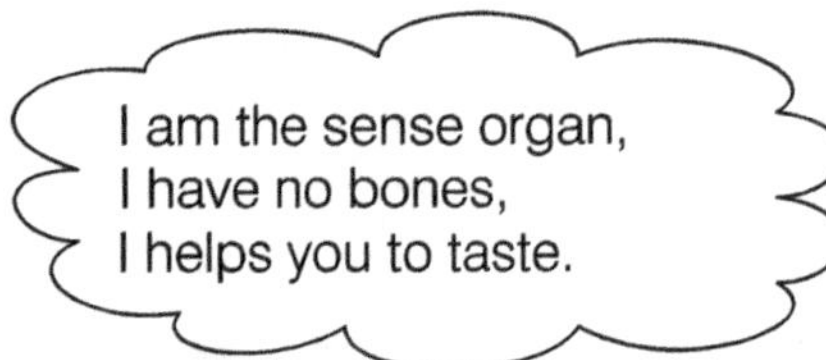

Who am I?
(a) Eyes (b) Tongue (c) Skin (d) Ear

13. Which of the following organ is called storehouse of food?
(a) Stomach (b) Lungs (c) Heart (d) Brain

14. Which tastes among the following can human tongue detects?
(a) Sour (b) Sweet (c) Bitter (d) All of these

15. The main function of the given organ is

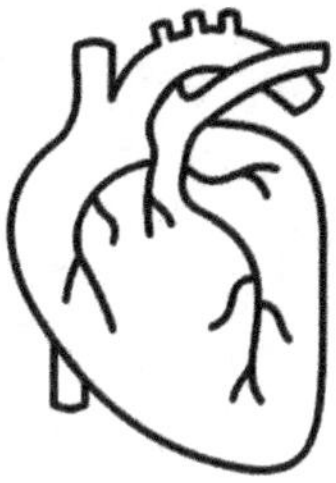

(a) to control all organs and body parts
(b) to digest food and give energy
(c) to pump blood in the whole body
(d) to give shape and support to body

16. The given organ is protected in

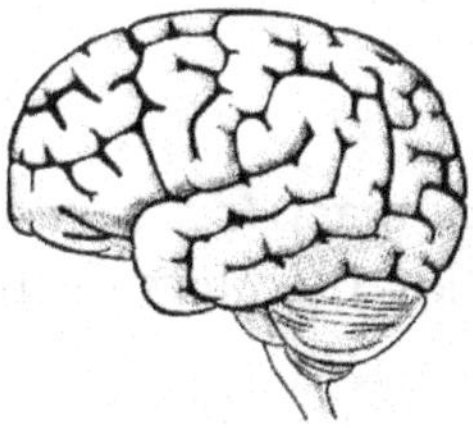

(a) Skull
(b) Heart
(c) Kidney
(d) Small intestine

17. Which of the following part is paired in our body?
(a) Eyes (b) Ears (c) Legs (d) All of these

18. Pick the incorrect statement.
(a) The skin helps us to feel things.
(b) The eyes help us to make (the difference of) colours and shapes.
(c) Muscles gives shape and support to our body.
(d) Our brain is protected by the skull.

19. The ...*A*... is a place in a human body where two bones meet.
(a) bone
(b) muscle
(c) lungs
(d) joint

20. Which of the following activity can be done without the use of hands?
(a) Cooking food
(b) Doing homework
(c) Watching cartoon
(d) Playing badminton

21. Our sense of ...... and ...... tell us that cloth is blue and soft.
(a) eyes and skin
(b) eyes and tongue
(c) skin and nose
(d) tongue and skin

22. Given organ helps you to remove waste material from your body. Identify organ.

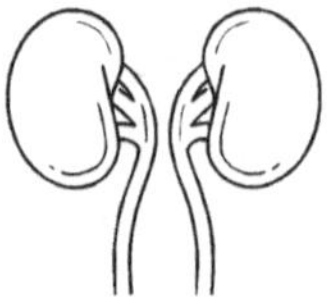

(a) Liver
(b) Lungs
(c) Stomach
(d) Kidney

23. Identify *P* and *Q*.

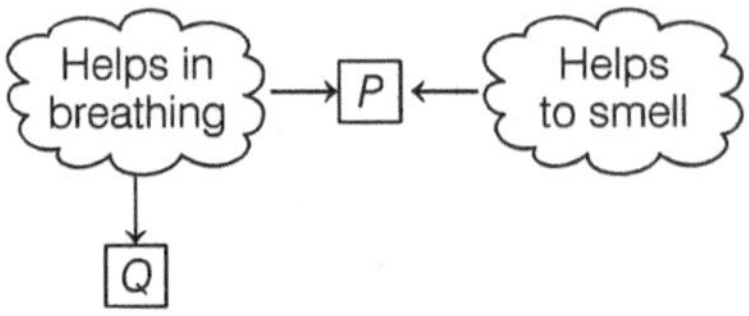

Choose the correct option.

	P	*Q*
(a)	Lungs	Heart
(b)	Nose	Lungs
(c)	Heart	Stomach
(d)	Lungs	Nose

24. Soniya was blind folded and her teacher asked her to differentiate some pairs of items. Which of the following pairs of items can she differentiate.

I. A cup of hot tea and a mug of cold coffee.
II. A piece of red cloth and a piece of blue cloth.

Choose the correct option.
(a) Only I
(b) Only II
(c) Both (a) and (b)
(d) None of these

25. Which organs are protected by these bones?

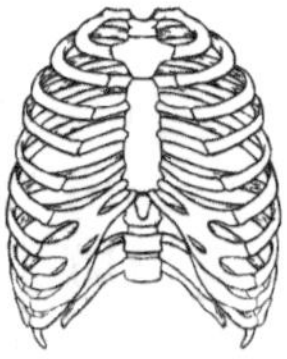

(a) Stomach
(b) Small intestine
(c) Liver
(d) Heart

Chapter

05

Food and Nutrition

- Food is the basic requirement of human body. We get food from plant as well as animals.
- Food helps us to grow, gives us energy, protects us from diseases, etc.
- Food contains nutrients like fat, carbohydrate, proteins, vitamins and minerals.

Types of Food

- Food rich in fat and carbohydrates are called as **energy giving food**. Fat rich food are butter, ghee, oil, etc., while carbohydrate, rich food are potato, rice, wheat, etc.
- Proteins helps us to build up our muscles. Foods rich in protein are called as **body building foods,** e.g. Egg, meat, pulses, soybean, etc.
- Vitamins and minerals help to protect our body from diseases. Foods rich in vitamins and minerals are **protecting foods,** e.g. All fruits and vegetables.
- We should eat all these three kinds of food in proper amount. This is known as balanced diet or proper diet.
- Person who eats only vegetables and other plant product are known as **vegetarian**.
- Person who eats meat and other animals flesh are known as **non-vegetarian**.

Healthy Eating Habits

Do's	Dont's
Wash hands before and after eating	Eat too much food
Chew food properly	Eat junk food
Eat healthy food	Eat with dirty hands
Eat meals at the proper time	Eat while watching T.V.

Let's Practice

1. The main sources of our food are
   (a) plants
   (b) animals
   (c) Both plants and animals
   (d) None of these

2. We get cereals, pulses, vegetables and nuts from
   (a) plants
   (b) animals
   (c) Both (a) and (b)
   (d) None of these

3. The given food items are sources of

Ghee

Butter

Potato

Rice

Wheat

   (a) proteins
   (b) vitamins and minerals
   (c) carbohydrates and fats
   (d) minerals

4. Fruits and vegetables provide us
   (a) proteins
   (b) carbohydrates
   (c) vitamins and minerals
   (d) fats

5. Food is necessary for us because
   (a) food helps us to grow
   (b) food gives us energy
   (c) food keeps us healthy
   (d) All of these

6. Which of these foods help us to grow?

Fruits

Bread

Rice

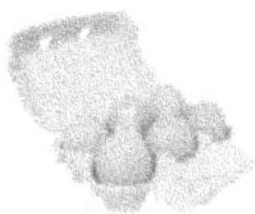
Eggs

Chicken

Milk

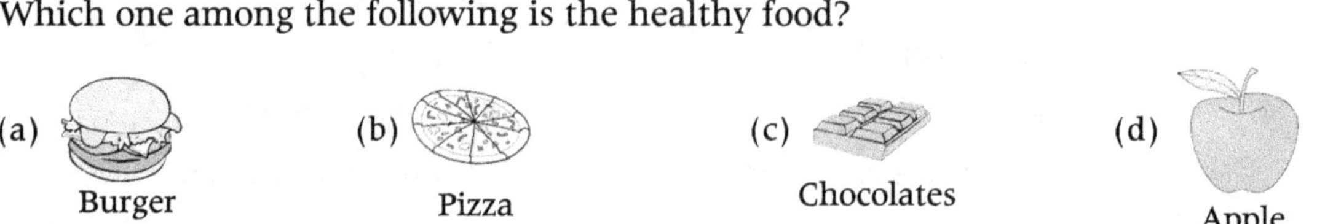

   (a) Fruits and bread
   (b) Fruits and rice
   (c) Eggs and rice
   (d) Eggs, chicken and milk

7. Which one among the following is the healthy food?

(a) 
Burger

(b) 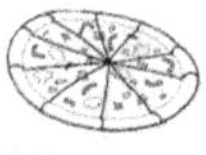
Pizza

(c) 
Chocolates

(d) 
Apple

8. Which of the following is/are protective food?

(a) 
Apple

(b) 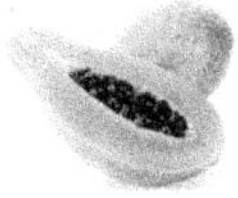
Papaya

(c) 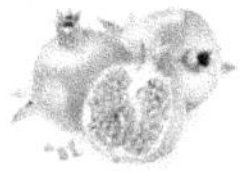
Pomegranate

(d) All of these

9. Neha get tired after playing badminton. Which of the following items give her energy?

(a) Rice and chapaties
(b) Eggs and chicken
(c) Spinach and tomato
(d) Rice and spinach

10. Which of the following pair is incorrectly matched?

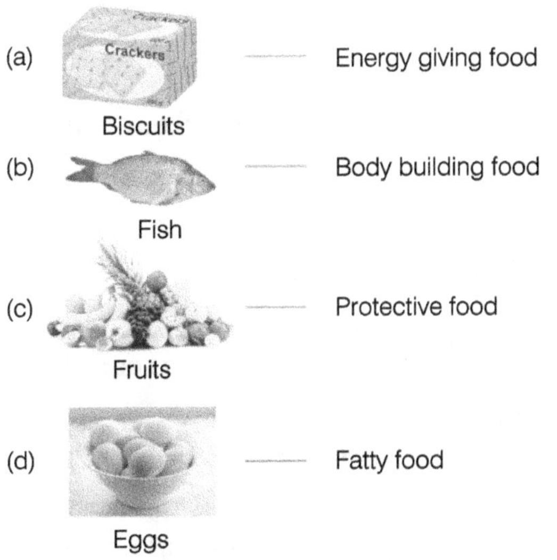

(a) 

Biscuits — Energy giving food

(b) 
Fish — Body building food

(c) 
Fruits — Protective food

(d) 
Eggs — Fatty food

11. People who eat fish, meat and chicken are called
(a) vegetarian
(b) non-vegetarian
(c) carnivorous
(d) omnivorous

12. Mummy says us to eat green vegetables like spinach because they are
(a) protective foods
(b) body building foods
(c) energy giving foods
(d) None of these

13. Match the following columns.

Column I		Column II
A.		1. Protein
B.	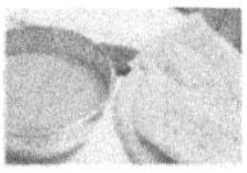	2. Junk food
C.		3. Calcium
D.		4. Carbohydrate

Codes

	A	B	C	D		A	B	C	D
(a)	4	3	2	1	(b)	3	4	1	2
(c)	3	4	2	1	(d)	4	3	1	2

14. Among the given food items, write the items which are obtained from plants.

Bread

Tomato soup

Omelette

Chicken

Chick peas

Milk

(a) Bread, tomato soup, omelette
(b) Bread, tomato soup, milk
(c) Chick peas, milk
(d) Chick peas, tomato soup , bread

15. Which of the following food can be eaten raw?
(a) Rice (b) Wheat (c) Cucumber (d) Egg

16. Balanced diet contains
(a) only junk food
(b) junk food and healthy food
(c) only healthy food with proper amount
(d) only junk food with proper amount

17. Mark ☺ if true and ☹, if false for the given statements.
I. Wash fruits and vegetables before eating. II. Cereals are animals products.
III. All vegetables should be taken as raw.

Codes

	I	II	III
(a)	☺	☺	☺
(b)	☺	☺	☹
(c)	☺	☹	☹
(d)	☹	☹	☹

18. Study the following chart

Protein rich food	Fat rich food	Carbohydrate rich food
Egg, Meat	Butter, Orange	Potato, Rice

Which of the following is under wrong heading?

(a) Meat (b) Orange (c) Potato (d) Rice

19. Look at the picture shown below.

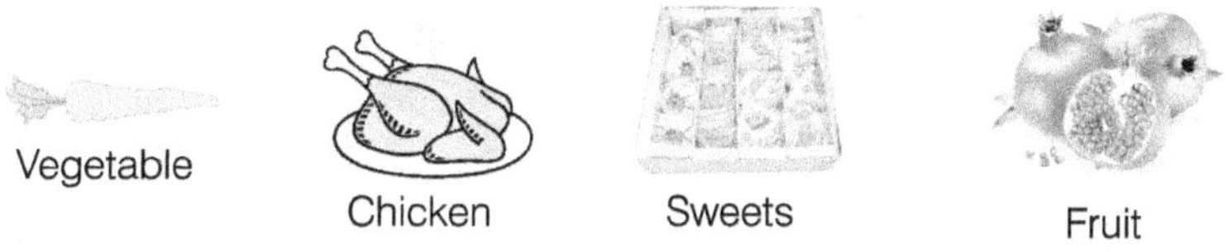

Place the given items in correct box.

	Energy giving food	Body building food	Protective food
(a)	Vegetable chicken	Sweets	Fruit
(b)	Sweets	Chicken	Vegetable, fruit
(c)	Vegetable	Sweets	Chicken, fruit
(d)	Fruits	Vegetable, sweets	Chicken

20. Some food items are eaten raw. They keep our body healthy. If these food items are cooked, then what will happen?

(a) They will become poisonous (b) Their protective nutrients may be lost due to heat

(c) They will get spoiled (d) None of these

21. Solve the given riddle.

I am a complete food,
I makes your bones strong,
A newborn baby drinks only me.

Who am I ?

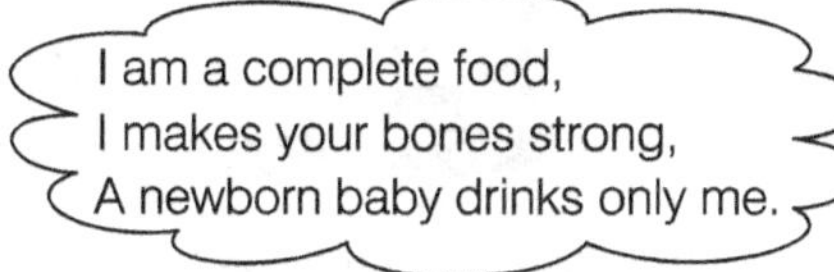

(a) Water (b) Juice (c) Milk (d) Soup

22. Read the following statement of *P* and *Q*

P: I am the richest source of protein for non-vegetarians

Q: I am the richest source of protein for vegetarians

Who is *P* and *Q* ?

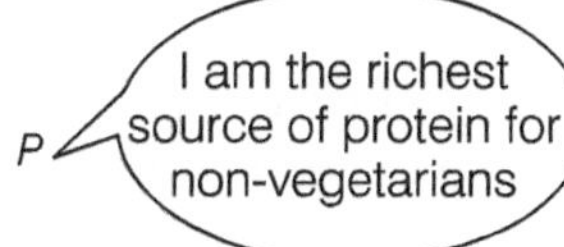

	P	*Q*		*P*	*Q*
(a)	Egg	Meat	(b)	Soybean	Wheat
(c)	Meat	Rice	(d)	Egg	Soybean

Chapter 06

Housing and Clothing

Houses

- The place where we live is called house. It protects us from heat, rain, cold, wild animals, etc.
- Materials required to build houses are bricks, iron, wood, cement, steel, etc.
- There are different rooms in a house, i.e. bedroom, living room, dining room, bathroom, kitchen, store room, etc.

Different Kinds of Houses

Kutcha House

It is made up of mud, straw and wood, e.g. Hut.

Pucca House

These houses are made up of bricks, cement and iron, e.g. Bungalow, buildings, etc.

Stilt House

These houses are made up of bomboo stilts. These houses are made in areas where rains heavily.

Igloos

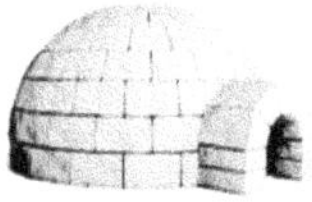

These houses are present in colder regions.These are made up of blocks of ice.

Tent

(It is made up of canvas cloth. It is used by campers, soldiers, etc.)

Houseboat

It is floating house made up of wood and ropes.

Clothes

- Clothes are made up of fibres.
- Fibres which we get from plants and animals are called **natural fibres**, e.g. Cotton, silk, wood and while fibres which prepared artificially are called **synthetic** or **man made fibre**, e.g. Nylon, rayon, etc.
- Clothes are wear according to seasons, occasions, occupation, etc.
- Clothes used in summer, winter and rainy season are cotton, woolen and waterproof, respectively.

Let's Practice

1. Which one of the following is a strong house?

(a)  (b)  (c) 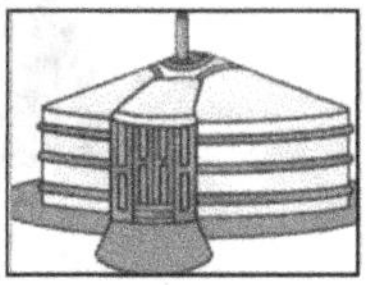 (d) 

2. Some houses are made from blocks of ice. Such houses are called
   (a) kutcha house
   (b) pucca house
   (c) igloo
   (d) caravan house

3. Which house is made up of cloth?
   (a) Tent
   (b) Caravan
   (c) Houseboat
   (d) Kutcha house

4. House provides us...... .
   (a) food
   (b) cloth
   (c) protection
   (d) All of these

5. The following types of clothes protect us from

   (a) summer
   (b) winter
   (c) rain
   (d) All of these

6. Complete the statement.

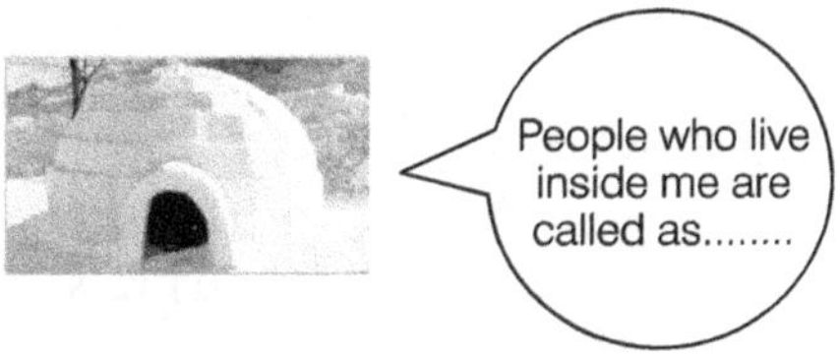

   (a) Eskimos
   (b) Gypsies
   (c) Campers
   (d) Wild animals

7. Match the clothes with the season you would wear in

Column I (Clothes)		Column II (Seasons)
A.		1. Summer
B.		2. Winter
C.		3. Rainy

Codes

	A	B	C		A	B	C
(a)	2	1	3	(b)	1	2	3
(c)	3	2	1	(d)	2	3	1

8. We wear cotton and light colour clothes in summer as
(a) they keep our body warm
(b) they absorbs heat
(c) they keep our body cool
(d) do not absorb sweat

9. Which of the following materials is not used to build a kutcha house?

Kutcha house

(a) Bamboo
(b) Cement
(c) Straw
(d) Grass

10. Purpose of building walls is to support roofs and ceilings.
The buildings material which is mainly used in constructions of walls is
(a) cement
(b) wood
(c) rubber
(d) plastic

11. Houseboats are mainly found in ...... and ......
(a) Kashmir and Kerala
(b) Kerala and Punjab
(c) Gujarat and Assam
(d) Kashmir and Punjab

12. Which of the following do not present in our house?
(a) Bedroom
(b) Kitchen
(c) Playground
(d) Bathroom

13. Mark , if true and , if false for the given statements.

I. Kutcha houses are strong.
II. A hut is made up of blocks of ice.

Codes

	I	II		I	II
(a)			(b)		
(c)			(d)		

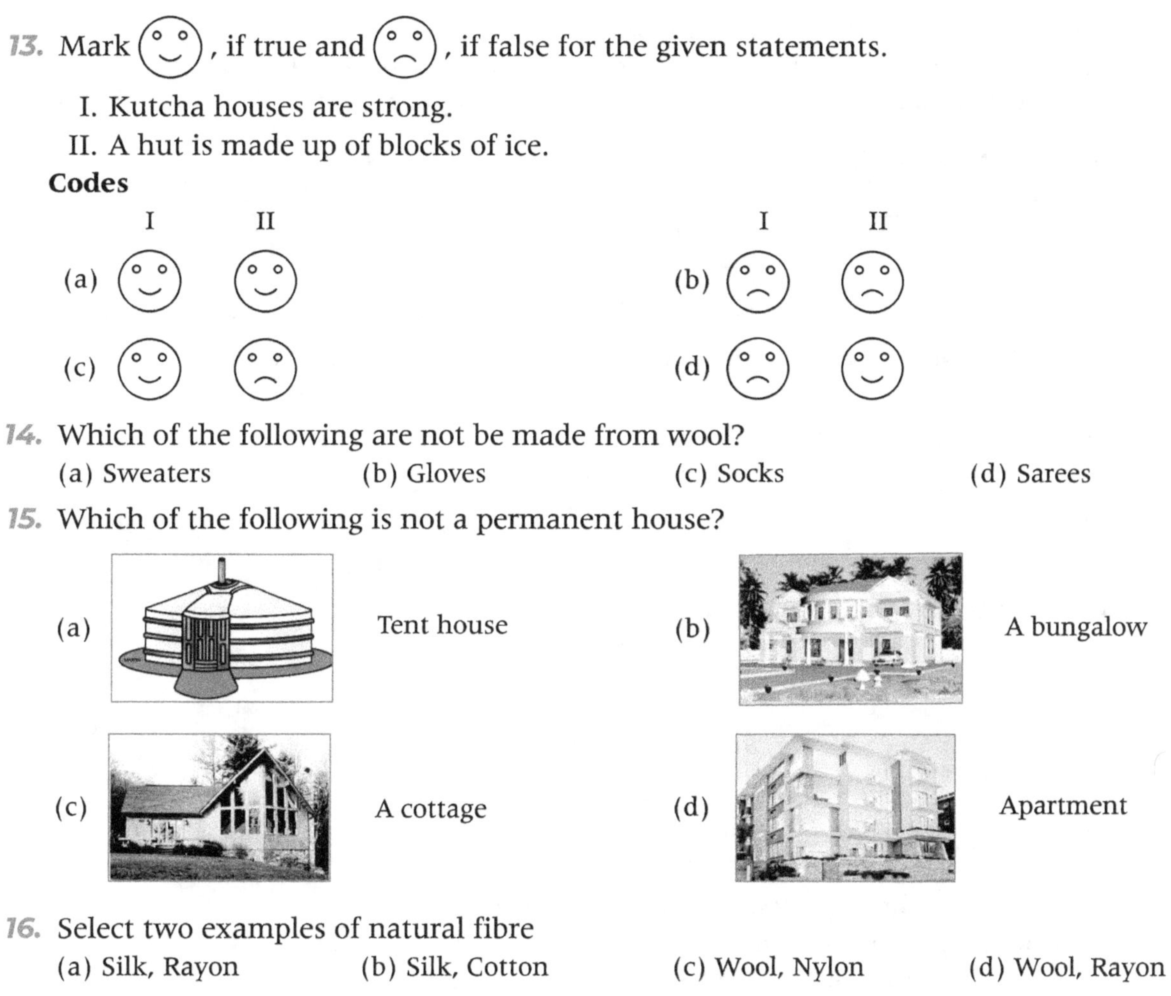

14. Which of the following are not be made from wool?
(a) Sweaters (b) Gloves (c) Socks (d) Sarees

15. Which of the following is not a permanent house?

(a) 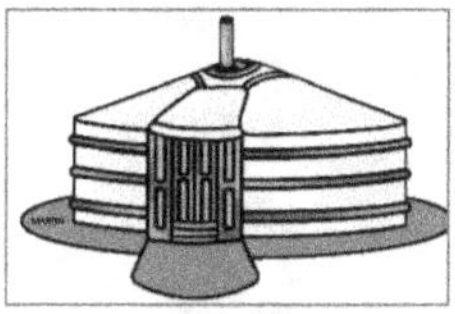 Tent house

(b)  A bungalow

(c)  A cottage

(d)  Apartment

16. Select two examples of natural fibre
(a) Silk, Rayon (b) Silk, Cotton (c) Wool, Nylon (d) Wool, Rayon

17. Match the following columns.

	Column I		Column II
A.	Mobile house	1.	Houseboat
B.	Floating-house	2.	Igloo
C.	Dome-shaped house	3.	Caravan

Codes

	A	B	C		A	B	C
(a)	1	2	3	(b)	3	1	2
(c)	3	2	1	(d)	1	3	2

18. Nylon ropes are widely available, nylon is
(a) a kind of natural cotton
(b) a kind of natural silk
(c) man- made fibre
(d) All of these

19. Which of the following statement is incorrect?
(a) Houses in the hills have sloping roofs
(b) A cottage is a small house
(c) All houses are build of mud only
(d) Houses in the plains have flat roof

20. Match the following columns.

	Column I		Column II
A.	A fabric that keeps us cool in summer	1.	Waterproof
B.	Hair of animals used to make clothes	2.	Cotton
C.	A material which does not let water to pass through	3.	Wool

Codes

	A	B	C		A	B	C
(a)	1	2	3	(b)	2	3	1
(c)	3	2	1	(d)	3	1	2

21. Choose the correct option on the basis of given picture.

(a) we wear sweaters, gloves, etc., to keep ourselves warm
(b) cold, dry air blows in winter season
(c) we sometimes light fire to keep us warm
(d) All of the above

22. Which of the following statements are correct about the house given below?

(a) These houses are raised from the ground level on bamboo stilts
(b) These houses are made in areas, where it rains heavily
(c) This does not let the water or snakes enter the house
(d) All of the above

23. Look at the picture carefully and choose the correct option.

(a) They have many homes in one building
(b) Each of them is called a flat
(c) These houses are very strong and are made from bricks, cement and steel
(d) All of the above

24. Rahul prepared list of temporary houses, while preparing he forget the name of our house. He only remembers that our house is called as house on wheels.

According to you, what is the name of the house?
(a) Caravan (b) Tent
(c) Houseboat (d) Pucca house

Chapter
07

Safety and First Aid

- Take bath daily.
- Brush your teeth twice a day.
- Wash your hands before and after eating.
- Eat only home cooked food. Avoid junk food.
- Always cover your mouth and nose, while sneezing and coughing.
- Always follow safety rules to avoid harms.Do not bite your nails.

Safety Rules

At Home
- Do not play with sharp objects like knife, scissors, etc.
- Do not touch hot object, matchsticks, gas cylinders, plugs, electric switches, etc.

On Road
- Always use zebra crossing while crossing the road.
- Obey the traffic light, i.e. red (stop), yellow (wait) and green (go).
- Always walk on footpath.

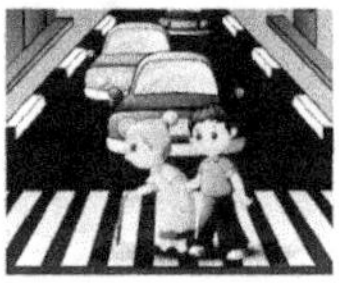

At School
- Do not stand on desk or chairs.
- Do not run or push someone on the stairs.

On Playground
- Do not throw waste anywhere, always use dustbin.
- Do not push or pull others while playing.
- Follow the rules of games while playing.

First Aid

- First aid is the immediately medical help given to an injured or sick person before doctors arrives.
- If a person get cut or bite by animal, wash the wound with soap and water then apply antiseptic cream.

Let's Practice

1. We should follow safety rules
   (a) only at homes
   (b) only at school
   (c) only on road
   (d) everywhere we go
2. The given picture show the symbol of

   (a) playground
   (b) hospital
   (c) danger
   (d) jungle
3. If you play with a knife or scissors you might get
   (a) a burn
   (b) a shock
   (c) a diseases
   (d) a cut
4. Which one of the following safety rules one must follow, while travelling in a school bus?

   (a) 

Getting off from a moving bus

   (b) 

Placing hands out of the vehicle

   (c) 

Disturbing the driver while driving

   (d) 
Getting into the bus in a queue

5. What is pedestrian crossing?
   (a) White and black strips on the road for safe crossing
   (b) It is a place where vehicles can park
   (c) It is a path were pedestrian can walk
   (d) It is a crossing where zebras cross
6. Draw , if statement is true and , if statement is false.

I. Swing on windows.
II. Play on road
III. Hold hands of parents on roads
IV. Obey traffic lights.

Codes

I II III IV
(a) 

I II III IV
(b) 

(c) 

(d) 

7. While riding a bicycle on the road, one should always keep

(a) to the right of the roadside
(b) in the middle of the road
(c) to the North of the road
(d) to the left of the roadside

8. Match the children with the safety rule they need to follow.

Column I	Column II
A. 	1. Getting into the bus in a queue
B. 	2. Cross the road at the zebra crossing
C. 	3. Walk on the footpath
D. 	4. Use footbridge to cross the road

Codes

	A	B	C	D
(a)	3	4	1	2
(b)	3	4	2	1
(c)	4	3	2	1
(d)	4	3	1	2

9. When somebody gets hurt, we need to help that person immediately. This immediate helps is called
(a) first aid
(b) last aid
(c) safety aid
(d) second aid

10. We should not touch electric switches with
(a) dry hands
(b) bare hands
(c) wet hands
(d) left hand

11. Which is not a good habit?
    (a) Talking to strangers
    (b) Brush your teeth twice a day
    (c) Share your lunch with your friends
    (d) Always obey elders

12. The main aim of giving first aid is to
    (a) save lives
    (b) keep the person comfortable till medical help arrives
    (c) Both (a) and (b)
    (d) None of the above

13. Which of the following should not be done on a staircase ?

    (a) We should not push or pull other children for fun
    (b) We should not lean over the railing of staircase
    (c) We should rush down the staircase
    (d) We should climb the steps in a line

14. Solve the given riddle.
    I am present with you in your school and your mother keep me at home or while travelling. Cotton, scissor, band-aid, antiseptic lotion, etc., are all my friends.
    Who am I?
    (a) Briefcase
    (b) First-aid box
    (c) Makeup box
    (d) None of these

15. Choose the correct option.
    We should not talk on mobile
    (a) while watching movie
    (b) when in a metro
    (c) while driving
    (d) when on the footpath

16. Select the items with which you can play in playground?

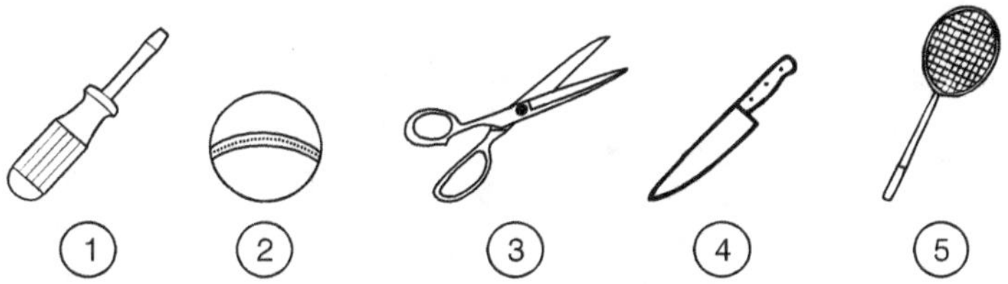

    (a) Only 2
    (b) 3, 4 and 5
    (c) 1, 2 and 3
    (d) 2 and 5

17. Which first aid treatment does not matched carrectly?
(a) Burning – rub ice on affected area
(b) Faint – make the person liedown
(c) Dog's bite – apply antiseptic lotion immediately
(d) Cut – apply bandage

18. In which of the following activities children are following safety rules?

(a)  (b)  (c)  (d) 

19. We should fly kites

(a) on the terrace
(b) in open grounds
(c) in school grounds
(d) on the road

20. Ram's mother will go out of town for some days. She prepares to do list for Ram at home

	Do's		Don'ts
A.	Cut your nails with nail cutter	D.	Bite your nails
B.	Clean ear with earbuds	E.	Comb your hair daily
C.	Switch off T.V plug after watching	F.	Lick your fingers after eating

Which one activity is under incorrect heading?
(a) Only E (b) Only B (c) Only A (d) Only F

21. Which of the following traffic signal indicate that the pedestrian must not cross the road?

Pedestrian lights

(a) When pedestrian light is green
(b) When pedestrian light is red
(c) When traffic light is red
(d) When traffic light is yellow

Chapter

08

Air, Water and Weather

Air

- Air is present all around us. We cannot see air but we can feel when it moves. Moving air is called **wind.**
- Air is a mixture of gases like carbon dioxide, oxygen, nitrogen, etc.
- It also contains some particles of dust and smoke.
- Moving air is **wind**. Gently moving wind is called **breeze** and strong and damaging wind is called **storm**.

Water

- Like air, water is also needed by all living organism. It is used for drinking, bathing, cooking, etc.
- We get water from rainwater. Rainwater fills oceans, lakes, etc.
- Some water seeps into the ground and is known as **groundwater**.We draw water from ground by **tubewell**, **handpump** and **well**.

Weather

- Weather is the daily condition of atmosphere of a particular place at particular time. It changes on daily basis conditions of sunshine, wind, rain, etc.
- Depending on weather, there are five seasons in India.

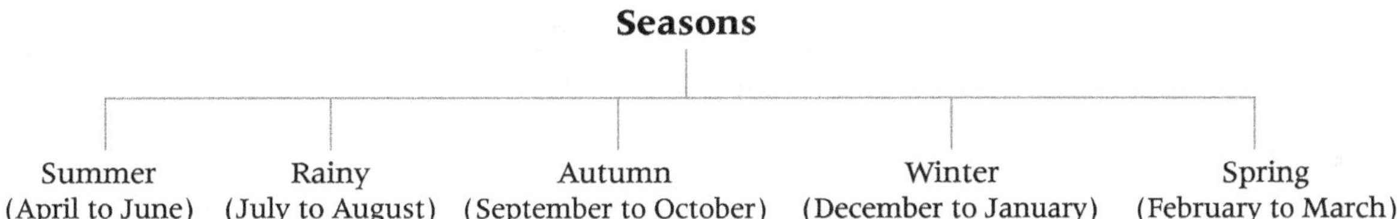

Seasons

Summer	Rainy	Autumn	Winter	Spring
(April to June)	(July to August)	(September to October)	(December to January)	(February to March)

Let's Practice

1. Look at the pictures given below

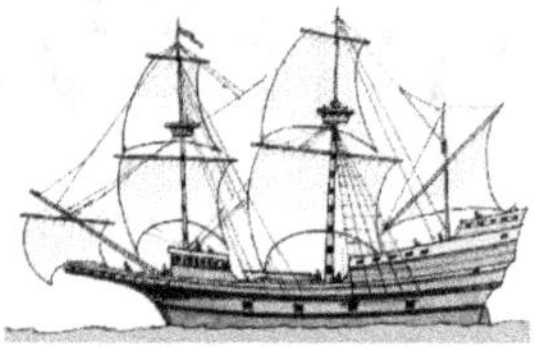

Sail boat

Windmill

Which is the common thing, they both need?

(a) Water (b) Wind (c) Sun (d) Wings

2. Which of the following is not a source of drinking water?

(a) 

Well

(b) 

Hand pump

(c) 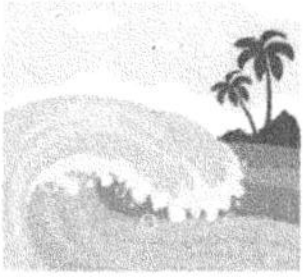

Seas and oceans

(d) 

Rainwater

3. How many seasons are there in India?

(a) 4 (b) 5 (c) 6 (d) 7

4. Match the following columns.

	Column I		Column II
A.	Breeze	1.	Healthy
B.	Water vapour	2.	Gentle wind
C.	Clean air	3.	Present in air
D.	Hottest season	4.	Summer

Codes

	A	B	C	D		A	B	C	D
(a)	2	3	1	4	(b)	3	1	2	4
(c)	3	4	1	2	(d)	4	3	1	2

5. Which of the following cannot be seen?
(a) Water (b) Flowers (c) Air (d) Mountains

6. Boiled water is better than normal water because boiling kills,
(a) microbes (b) soil (c) nutrients (d) chlorine

7. In which season you see rainbows?
(a) Autumn (b) Winter (c) Rainy (d) Spring

8. Which is the incorrect match?

	Column I	Column II
(a)	Coldest season	Winter
(b)	It fills up ponds, lakes, rivers and seas	Rain water
(c)	This gives us water in our home	Tap
(d)	We do this to kill germs in water	Freezing

9. Look at the information given below.
Dust and smoke comes from cars and factories. This conditions makes air… .
(a) clean (b) polluted (c) fresh (d) germ free

10. Which season comes in November to January?
(a) Winter (b) Spring (c) Summer (d) Rainy

11. Match the following columns.

	Column I		Column II
A.	Gumboots	1.	Weight
B.	Air	2.	Rainy season
C.	Windmill	3.	Ice
D.	Solid form of water	4.	Produce electricity

Codes

	A	B	C	D
(a)	4	2	3	1
(b)	2	1	4	3
(c)	3	4	1	2
(d)	1	3	2	4

12. Which of the following things can be done to keep the air clean and fresh?

(a) 

(b) 

(c) 

(d) All of these

13. Figure represent water cycle

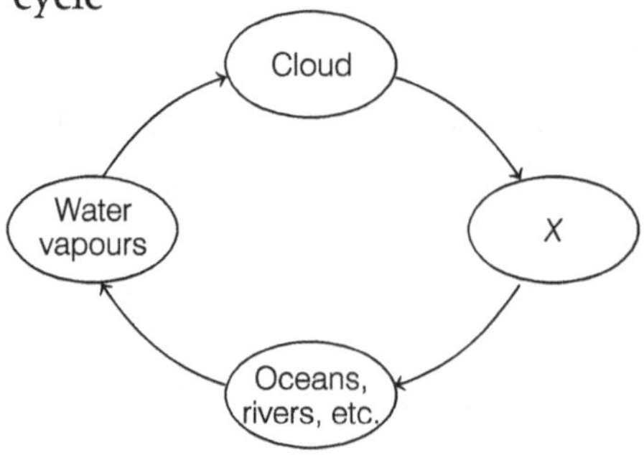

Identify *X*.

(a) Rain (b) Sun (c) Bird (d) Mountain

14. In which season trees shed their leaves?

(a) Autumn (b) Spring (c) Summer (d) Winter

15. Which of the following statement is incorrect?

(a) Air is needed for survival of human beings, plants and animals
(b) Moving air is called wind
(c) Air contains dust and smoke only
(d) Air has weight

16. Mark ☺, if true statement and ☹, if false statement.

I. Drinking water should be stored in clean vessels.
II. Containers with drinking water should be covered.
III. It is not our duty to save every drop of water

	I	II	III
(a)	☺	☺	☺
(b)	☹	☹	☹
(c)	☺	☺	☹
(d)	☺	☹	☹

17. Umbrella is used in which season?

(a) Summer (b) Rainy (c) Both (a) and (b) (d) Autumn

18. Look at the figure given below.
All these activities shows that air

Air filled in a balloon

Air filled in tyre

(a) has weight
(b) occupies space
(c) contains water vapour
(d) contains dust only

19. Solve the given riddle.
I am a beautiful words season,
Flowers bloom everywhere,
When I come,
Who am I ?
(a) Spring (b) Winter (c) Autumn (d) Summer

20. Three students were talking about the air around us
Sonal— The air in my school bottle is sweet.
Ritu— Air in my room is blue.
Anu—Air in my room is cool.
Whose statement is correct about air?
(a) Sonal (b) Ritu
(c) Anu (d) All statements are correct

21. Look at the picture and tell us the three forms of water?

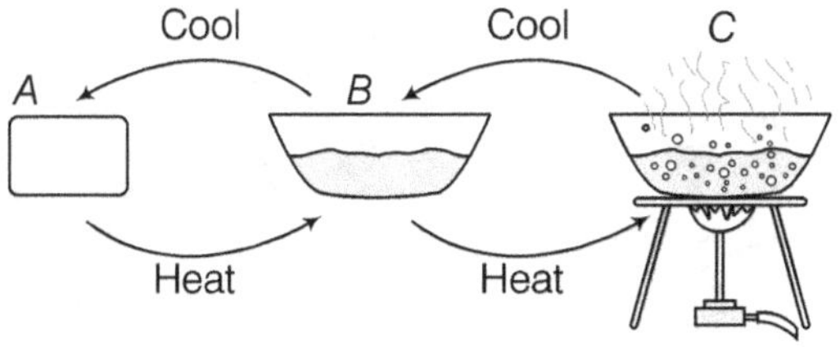

Codes

	A	B	C
(a)	Ice	Water	Water vapour
(b)	Water vapour	Water	Ice
(c)	Water	Ice	Water vapour
(d)	Water vapour	Ice	Water

22. Ramu's teacher light a candle and placed it on a table. Simultaneously, she took another candle in a wide container then she light it and cover it with a glass. The flame of the candle covered with glass blows out after some time.

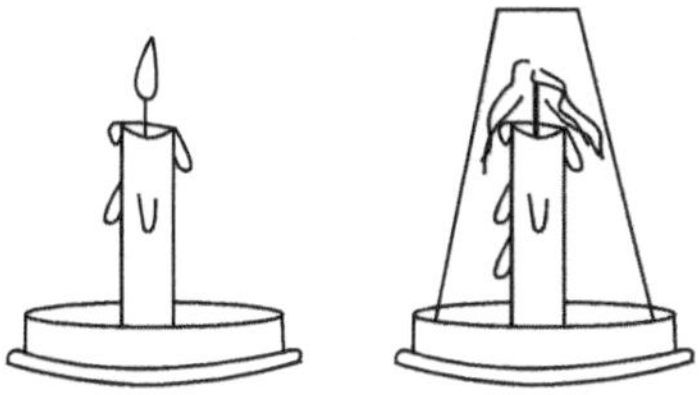

What does this experiment shows?
(a) Candle cannot burn for long time (b) Air has weight
(c) Air is needed for burning (d) None of these

23. Water drops fall from the clouds as rain. Where does rain water go?

I. It filled oceans and seas.
II. It get absorbed by plants.
III. It goes down in ground.

Codes

(a) Only I
(b) Only II
(c) I and III
(d) I, II and III

24. Suman read the weather forecast of coming week in her city

Monday	Tuesday	Wednesday	Thursday	Friday

Which of the following items, she should buy in such a weather?

(a) Raincoat, umbrella, gumboots
(b) Sunglasses, new clothes, plastic bottle
(c) Raincoat, woolen socks, woolen gloves
(d) Umbrella, heaters, sunglasses

Chapter
09

Our Surroundings

- **Our family**, neighbourhood, plants and animals together make our surroundings.
- A family is a group of people that are related to each other. People who lives together in a family are called **family members** like grandparents, mother, uncle, aunt, etc.
- All these family members may or may not live in the same house.
- If only parents and their children live together in the same house, it is called **nuclear family.**

- If children, their parents, grandparents or other relatives live together in the same house, it is called **joint family.**

Neighbourhood

Neighbourhood means the area near or around our houses like police station, railway station, post office, etc.

Occupation

- Different people do different kind of jobs in our neighbourhood to earn money.
- A person doing any kind of job is known as its **occupation**.
- Examples of people having different occupations are lawyer, postman, milkman, etc.

Let's Practice

1. Which one of the following is a traffic inspector?

(a) 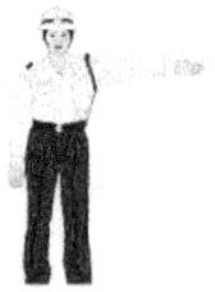 (b)  (c)  (d) 

2. Ritu is a .... She stitches clothes.
   (a) security guard (b) doctor (c) cobbler (d) tailor
3. The family in the given picture is of a

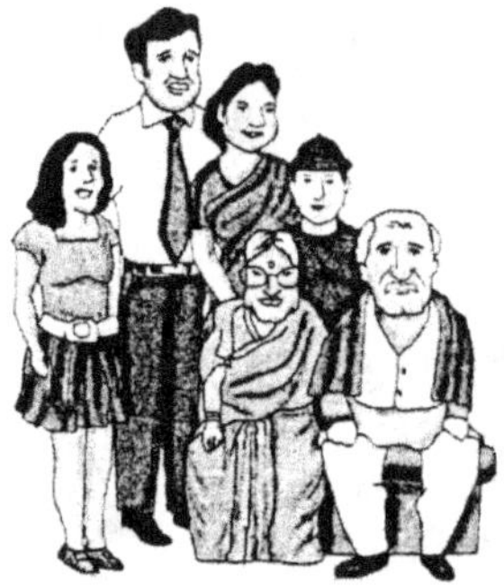

   (a) Joint family (b) Small nuclear family
   (c) Large nuclear family (d) None of these
4. Keshav wants to have cool haircut for a party. Which of the following person will help him?
   (a) Barber (b) Policeman (c) Tailor (d) Nurse
5. Who among the following comes to your house everyday?
   (a) Policeman (b) Newspaper hawker
   (c) Milkman (d) Both (b) and (c)
6. Sarita has to buy medicines for her brother. She should go to a ...
   (a) greengrocer (b) chemist (c) florist (d) baker
7. Which of the following family members is not a part of a nuclear family?
   (a) Grandmother (b) Grandfather (c) Cousin (d) All of these
8. You are going to hill station with your family for summer vacation. Who will take care of the safety of your house in your absence?
   (a) Watchman (b) Carpenter (c) Policeman (d) Soldier
9. Your uncle's son is your ....
   (a) cousin (b) nephew (c) niece (d) uncle

10. Who will used to following tools?

(a) Potter (b) Cobbler (c) Tailor (d) Carpenter

11. Who among the following will not help to build a house?
(a) Plumber (b) Barber (c) Electrician (d) Carpenter

12. Which sign is used on a ambulance van?
(a) + (b) – (c) | (d) ×

13. ...... station is the junction of trains.
(a) Police (b) Railway (c) Fire (d) Radio

14. If you are looking for a doctor, where will you go?
(a) Police station (b) Hospital (c) Post office (d) Court

15. Which of the following thing a tailor will not need to do his work?
(a) Comb (b) Scissors (c) Inch tape (d) Clothes

16. Who is the man in the given figure?
(a) Postman
(b) Policeman
(c) Doctor
(d) Pilot

17. A person does a job to ......
(a) earn money (b) spent time (c) enjoy (d) play games

18. Match the following columns.

	Column I		Column II
A.	Kalpana Chawala	1.	Cricketer
B.	M. S. Dhoni	2.	Prime Minister
C.	Narendra Modi	3.	Scientist
D.	Abdul Kalam	4.	Astronaut

Codes

	A	B	C	D
(a)	1	2	3	4
(b)	2	1	4	3
(c)	3	2	4	1
(d)	4	1	2	3

Direction (Q. 19 to 23) Solve the given crossward.

Across

19. ...... teaches in schools and colleges.
(a) Postman (b) Teacher (c) Soldier (d) Cobbler

20. ...... maintains law and order in cities.
(a) Policeman (b) Ecologist (c) Astronaut (d) Principal

21. ...... is in the army who wears uniform and has gun.
(a) Fireman (b) Teacher (c) Milkman (d) Soldier

Down

22. ...... grows crops, fruits and vegetables .
(a) Farmer (b) Lawyer (c) Barber (d) Doctor

23. ...... treats patients.
(a) Banker (b) Doctor (c) Driver (d) Dancer

24. Read the conversation between two friends. Which of the following persons should they visit ?

	Rahul	Ritu
(a)	Dentist	Plumber
(b)	Plumber	Stationer
(c)	Doctor	Stationer
(d)	Chemist	Doctor

25. Mrs. Rubi teaches Maths to you and her husband Mr. Ramesh bakes cake on your birthday. What are Mrs. Rubi and Mr. Ramesh occupations?
(a) Mrs. Rubi - Teacher, Mr. Ramesh - Baker (b) Mrs. Rubi - Doctor, Mr Ramesh - Teacher
(c) Mrs. Rubi - Writer, Mr. Ramesh Chemist (d) Mrs. Rubi - Nurse, Mr Ramesh - Carpenter

Chapter 10

Our Universe

- Our universe is made up of Sun, Moon, stars, comets, asteroids, different planets, etc.
- The Sun, the Moon and different planets together makes **our solar system**.

The Sun

- It is the brightest and nearest star to the Earth.
- It is the main source of light on Earth.
- It is present at the center of our solar system.
- It rises in the East and sets in the West.

The Moon

- It is the natural satellite of Earth.
- It moves around the Earth only.
- It does not has its own light.
- It is smaller than the Sun and the Earth.

Planets

- They moves around the Sun.
- In our solar system, there are eight planets at present namely; Mercury, Venus, Earth, Mars, Jupiter, Saturn, Uranus and Neptune.
- Earth is the only planet with life because it has air and water. It is also called as blue planet because about three-fourth part of land is covered with water. It is the third planet from the Sun.
- Mercury is a smallest planet, Jupiter is a biggest planet. Mars is a red planet and Saturn is ringed planet.

Space Travellers

- **Neil Armstrong** was the first man who land on the Moon.
- **Rakesh Sharma** was the first Indian man to go into the space.
- **Kalpana Chawla** was the first Indian woman to go into the space.

Shadow

- When an object does not allow a light to pass through it, a shadow of the object is formed.
- Shadow changes as the Earth moves.
- In evening and morning, shadows formed by the Sun are longer.
- At noons, shadows formed by the Sun are shorter.

Let's Practice

1. Our solar system has ...... planets.
   (a) 8 (b) 10 (c) 6 (d) 7

2. Look at the figure of solar system.

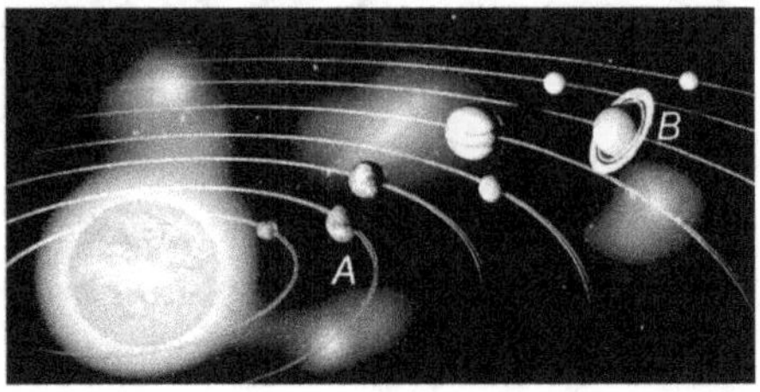

   Name the planet *B* in the solar system.
   (a) Neptune (b) Uranus (c) Saturn (d) Venus

3. Stars are ...... in the sky.
   (a) one thousand (b) one lakh (c) one crore (d) uncountable

4. Earth is also known as 'Blue planet' because of
   (a) air (b) water (c) land (d) gas

5. We can see tiny ......*A*...... in the sky.
   (a) planets (b) stars (c) comets (d) asteroids

6. The largest planet in our solar system is
   (a) Jupiter (b) Saturn (c) Neptune (d) Earth

7. Which is not a planet ?
   (a) Venus (b) Neptune (c) Saturn (d) Moon

8. Moon moves around the ....
   (a) Sun (b) Earth (c) Stars (d) Mars

9. Which of the following is wrongly matched?

(a)	Evening star	Venus
(b)	Red planet	Mars
(c)	Coldest planet	Neptune
(d)	Smallest planet	Saturn

10. Which of the following has light of its own?
    (a) The Moon (b) A planet (c) The Sun (d) A satellite

11. Who is the head of our solar system?
(a) The Earth (b) Jupiter (c) The Sun (d) The Moon

12. The Sun looks like a ......
(a) ball of fire (b) ball of football (c) ball of snow (d) ball of cricket

13. At which position, the Earth is placed in our solar system?
(a) Ist (b) IInd (c) IIIrd (d) IVth

14. The Sun rises in which direction?
(a) North (b) East (c) West (d) South

15. Look at the following figures, when length of the shadow changes during the day.

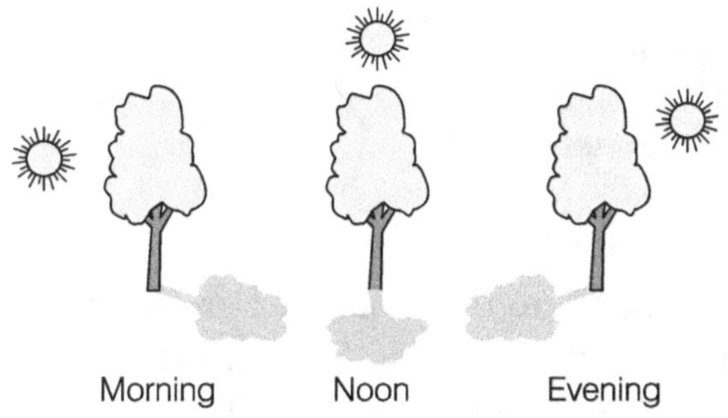

The shadow is formed is every time zone. At what time, the shadow will be longest?
(a) At noon (b) During morning
(c) During evening (d) Both during morning and evening

16. Which statement is wrong about Sun and star?
(a) They both are star (b) They have their own light
(c) They differ in shape (d) All statements are wrong

17. Look at the following picture. The person who travels in space is known as

(a) Robot (b) Astronaut
(c) Scientist (d) Geologist

18. Choose the incorrect statement
(a) Moon moves around the Earth
(b) Stars have light of its own
(c) Sun is the hottest planet
(d) Planets move around the Sun

19. We see different shapes of ...., every day.
(a) The Moon
(b) The Sun
(c) The Earth
(d) The Mercury

20. The following picture shows the eight planets of our solar system.

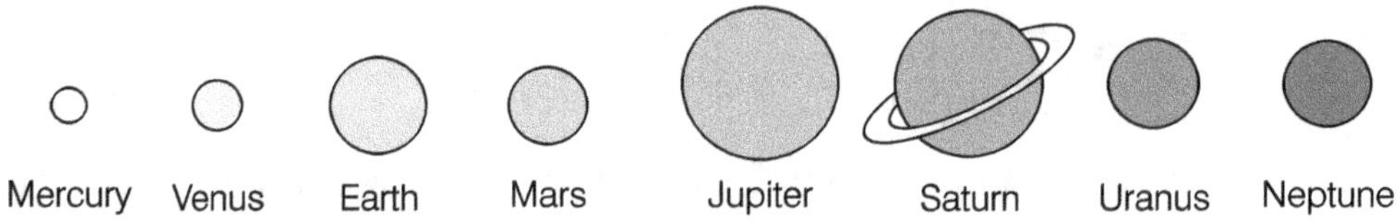

Choose the correct option.
(a) Planets have a light of their own
(b) They do not reflect the sunlight
(c) They give their light to the Earth
(d) Planets do not have a light of their own

21. Arrange the Earth, the Sun and the Moon in increasing order of their size.
(a) The Sun < The Moon < The Earth
(b) The Earth < The Moon < The Sun
(c) The Moon < The Earth < The Sun
(d) The Moon < The Sun < The Earth

22. Study the following chart carefully.

	Moves around the Sun	Part of our solar system	Have its own light
P	×	×	✓
Q	×	✓	×

Identify *P* and *Q*.

	P	*Q*
(a)	Moon	Earth
(b)	Star	Moon
(c)	Earth	Moon
(d)	Moon	Star

PRACTICE SET 01

1. The given food items are

(a) energy giving food (b) body-building food (c) protective food (d) roadside food

2. Arrange the following group in increasing order of their size.

Coconut tree	Rose plant	Mint plant

(a) Rose plant < Mint plant < Coconut tree (b) Coconut tree < Rose plant < Mint plant
(c) Mint plants < Rose plant < Coconut tree (d) Coconut tree < Mint plant < Rose plant

3. Write the name of the product that we get from the plants that are shown below.

A. Bamboo plant .... B. Rose plant .... C. Sugarcane plant ....

	A	*B*	*C*
(a)	Wood	Oil	Sugar
(b)	Wood	Seeds	Sugar
(c)	Paper	Perfumes	Sugar
(d)	Paper	Oil	Cloves

4. Which of the following statements is correct?
(a) It is always safe to play on the road.
(b) We must use the footpath while walking.
(c) When the traffic signal shows red, the vehicles should move.
(d) It is not necessary to obey all the traffic rules.

5. Give the one word for the following puzzle.
I help the leaves to rustle and pinwheel to turn. Who am I?
(a) Gale (b) Storm (c) Breeze (d) Rain

6. Which of the following yield fibre?

(a) 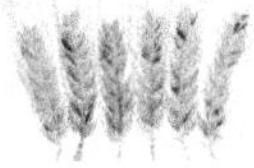
Barley

(b) 
Tea

(c) 
Cotton

(d) 
Mustard

7. The person in the given figure is a/an

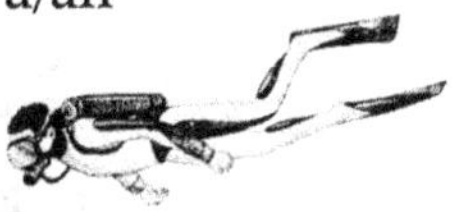

(a) doctor (b) soldier (c) diver (d) astronaut

8. Which part of the given plant produces seeds?

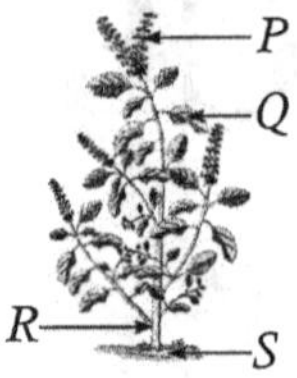

(a) *P* (b) *S* (c) *Q* (d) *R*

9. What causes water to change from one form to another?

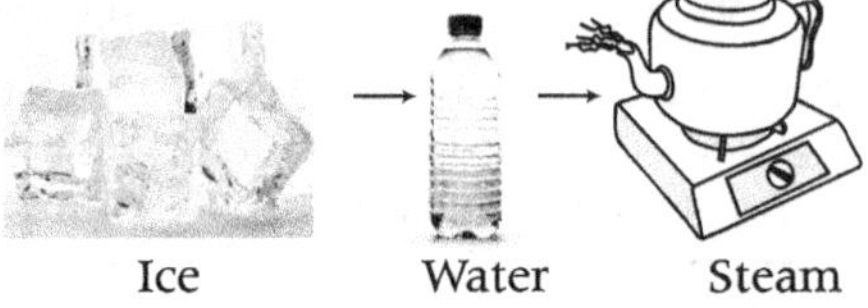

(a) Heating (b) Cooling (c) Heating and cooling (d) None of these

10. Look at the pictures given below. Match the plant with its correct type.

	Column I	Column II
A.		1. Herb
B.		2. Shrub
C.	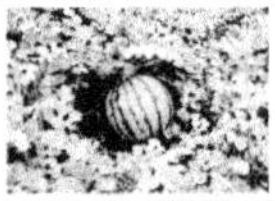	3 Tree
D.		4. Creeper

Codes

	A	B	C	D
(a)	4	3	2	1
(b)	3	4	2	1
(c)	3	1	4	2
(d)	4	2	1	3

11. A pond contains clean water. Which of the following activities will produce least pollution of water?
    (a) Washing clothes in the pond
    (b) Animals bathing in the pond
    (c) Washing motor vehicles in the pond
    (d) Swimming in the pond

12. Which of the following is incorrectly matched?
    (a)  Food stored in a fruit
    (b)  Food stored in a stem
    (c)  (wheat) Food stored in seeds
    (d) 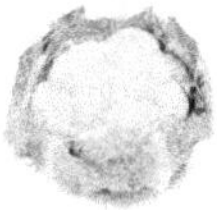 Food stored in flower

13. Which of the following tree gives us gum?
    (a) *Acacia* tree (b) Coconut tree (c) Banyan tree (d) Mango tree

14. Match the following columns.

	Column I		Column II
A.	Gorilla	1.	Cave
B.	Snake	2.	Den
C.	Tiger	3.	Hole
D.	Bear	4.	Open places

Codes

	A	B	C	D
(a)	4	3	1	2
(b)	2	1	3	4
(c)	1	3	2	4
(d)	4	3	2	1

15. Clothes take longer time to dry on a

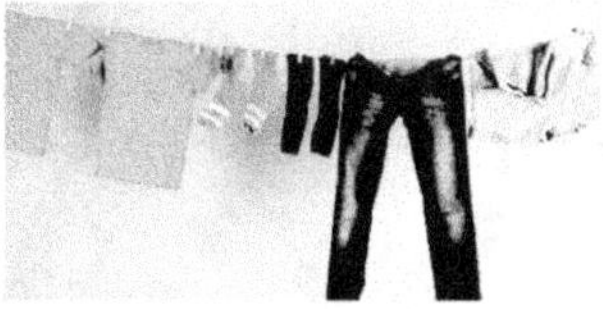

(a) sunny day (b) rainy day (c) dry day (d) windy day

16. Which of the following is not our sense organ?

(a) 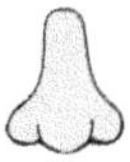 (b)  (c) 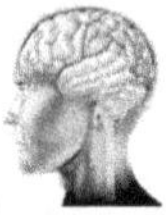 (d) 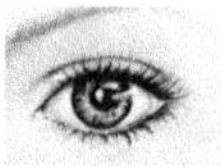

17. Name the body part which has all the sense organs present in it.

(a) Stomach (b) Heart
(c) Hands (d) Head

18. Match the animals with the things we get from them and mark the correct option.

	Column I		Column II
A.	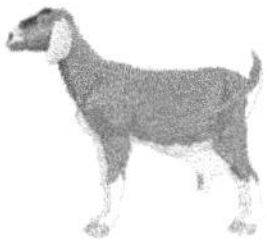	1.	
B.		2.	
C.	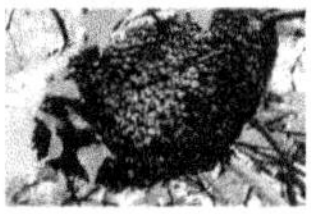	3.	
D.		4.	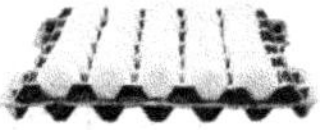

Codes

	A	B	C	D
(a)	4	3	1	2
(b)	3	4	1	2
(c)	3	1	2	4
(d)	3	1	4	2

19. Choose the correct option. What is posture?

(a) It is a soft part of our body which is below our skin
(b) It is the hard part of our body
(c) It is the position of our body while standing, sitting or walking
(d) It is the framework of bones

20. Fill in the blanks with the correct options.

I. The Sun gives us heat and ....
II. The half of the Earth that faces the Sun has ....
III. We have day and night because the ...... rotates.
IV. Moon shines in the light of the ... .

Codes

	I	II	III	IV
(a)	energy	day	Moon	Earth
(b)	day	night	Sun	Earth
(c)	light	day	Earth	Sun
(d)	energy	night	Earth	Sun

21. Which of the following animal does not eat the flesh of other animals?

(a)  (b)  (c)  (d) 

22. Which type of clothes would you prefer on a sunny day?
(a) Thick woollen clothes
(b) Raincoat
(c) Light cotton clothes
(d) Silk clothes

23. Sheela's teacher has arranged the apparatus shown below :

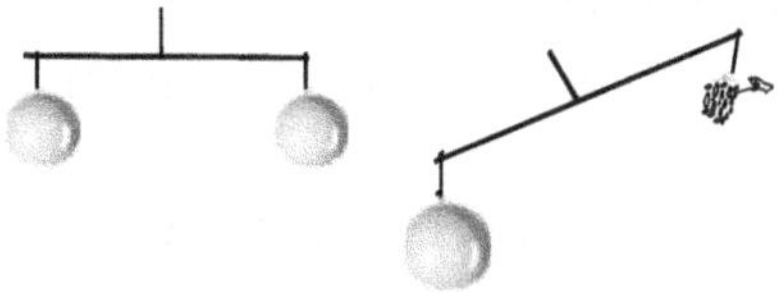

First she blow up two balloons and then she pricks a pin in one of the balloon.
What does Sheela's teacher want to convey?
(a) Air cannot be stored (b) Air is nothing (c) Air is a simply a gas (d) Air has weight

24. Which of the following activities is good for reducing air pollution?

(a)  (b)  (c)  (d) Both (a) and (b)

25. Electricity makes many things work in a house. It is also very powerful. What are methods one should not adopt as it can harm the person?

(a) 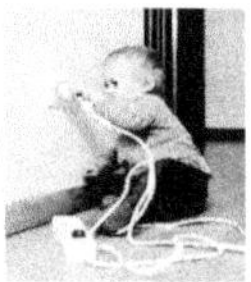
Play with electricity

(b) 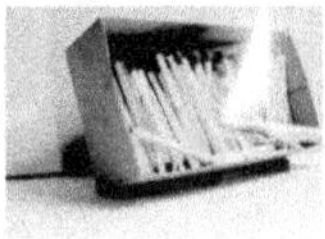
Do not play with fire

(c) 
Washing the floors

(d) None of these

26. Complete the following sentence. The main function of lungs is to take ...*A*... and give out ...*B*... and the process is known as ...*C*...

	A	*B*	*C*
(a)	carbon dioxide	oxygen	digestion
(b)	oxygen	carbon dioxide	digestion
(c)	oxygen	carbon dioxide	breathing
(d)	carbon dioxide	oxygen	breathing

27. Guess my name

These houses are built with sloping roofs, in places where it rains heavily. Who am I?

(a) Kutcha house (b) Cottage (c) Stilts (d) Yurt

28. Which of the following activities is a healthy eating habits?

(a) Washing hands before eating (b) Talking while eating food
(c) Eating stale food (d) Overeating

29. A house floating on a lake is called ....

(a) tents (b) house boat (c) caravans (d) None of these

30. How many planets revolve around the Sun in the solar system?

(a) 8 (b) 9 (c) 10 (d) 11

31. The smallest bone of the human body is present in

(a) nose (b) ear (b) mouth (d) None of these

32. What type of water, we need to drink?

(a) Saltwater (b) Freshwater (c) Polluted water (d) Bitter water

33. The process of photosynthesis takes place in the

(a) stem (b) leaves (c) root (d) flower

34. Ankur is suffering from cough and cold. He should visit a

(a) Plumber (b) Police station (c) Doctor (d) None of these

35. Most of the living organism's need .... to breathe.

(a) Nitrogen (b) Oxygen (c) Carbon dioxide (d) None of these

PRACTICE SET 02

1. What will happen to a plant if we remove all the flowers from it?
   (a) It will not produce fruits
   (b) It cannot stand upright on the ground
   (c) It will stop transporting food and water to all other parts
   (d) It will stop absorbing nutrients and water from the oil
2. We should never play with ....
   (a) blade (b) football (c) matchbox (d) Both (a) and (c)
3. Which is the smallest planet of our solar system?
   (a) Mercury (b) Venus (c) Earth (d) Neptune
4. Ishika eats too many chocolates and sweets everyday. This can cause cavities in her
   (a) Muscles (b) Eyes (c) Teeth (d) Lungs
5. Read the chart carefully.

Parts of plants	*X*	*Y*
Root	✓	✓
Stem	✓	✓
Leaves	✓	✓
Flower	✓	✓
Fruits	✓	×

   Identify *X* and *Y*

	X	*Y*		*X*	*Y*
(a)	Rose	Lotus	(b)	Mango	Apple
(c)	Orange	Rose	(d)	Papaya	Mango

6. Raj is married to Vaishnavi. Vaishnavi is .... of Raj.
   (a) Fiance (b) Mother (c) Sister (d) Wife
7. Rahul goes to school on a bicycle, which of these safety rules should be follow?
   (a) He should keep to the right of road
   (b) He should give signals before taking turns
   (c) He should cross the road by using zebra crossing
   (d) All of the above
8. *X* is the farthest planet from the Sun in our solar system. *X* is ....
   (a) Neptune (b) Jupiter (c) Saturn (d) Uranus

9. Select the odd one out on the basis of food group to which they belong.
(a) Fish (b) Egg (c) Bread (d) Chicken

10. Refer to what Harsh is saying.

Harsh — I love shining raindrops on leaves.

Which sense organ has to used for that?
(a) Ear (b) Eyes (c) Lips (d) Nose

11. Select the habit that we should not follow
(a) Overloading the load carrying animals
(b) Throwing stones at animals
(c) Tying fire crackers on the tail of stray animals
(d) All of these

12. Select the incorrect match.
(a) Sugar - Plant (b) Honey - Insect (c) Salt - Animal (d) Cocoa - Plant

13. Somya and Rishi was playing inside the house when Rishi fainted. Somya should...... .
(a) Take Atul under the Sun
(b) Tie bandage on Rishi's head
(c) Wrap Rishi in a blanket
(d) None of these

14. Which of the following is/are gaseous state(s) of water?
1. Water vapour 2. Rain 3. Snow 4. Dew
(a) Only 3 (b) Only 1 (c) 2, 3 and 4 (d) All of these

15. Which of these is taken in least amount in a healthy balanced diet?
(a) Butter and oil
(b) Fruits and vegetables
(c) Cereal, gram and pulses
(d) Egg, milk and yoghurt

16. Read the following groups, which of the following thing is wrongly placed?

Living things	**Non-living things**
Dog	Chair
Cat	Men
Plant	Computer

(a) Plant (b) Men (c) Computer (d) Dog

17. Solve the riddle given below.

It is a small bushy plant with hard stem and branches.
We get soft fibre from it, which is used for stuffing pillows.

Who am I?
(a) Jute plant (b) Cotton plant (c) Coconut plant (d) Money plant

18. Aman has difficulty in breathing. He may have some problem with his ....
(a) Lungs (b) Stomach (c) Liver (d) Kidney

19. Varun's house is built on wooden logs and its has sloping roofs. Varun most probably be residing in a place where ....
1. Floods are common
2. Heavy rainfall occurs
3. Forest fires are common
4. Earthquakes are common
(a) 1 and 4 only (b) 1 and 2 only (c) 2 and 3 only (d) 3 and 4 only

20. Which of the following should not be done while eating?
(a) Stuff your mouth
(b) Chew with mouth closed
(c) Chew food slowly
(d) Avoid talking

21. In hilly areas, houses are made with sloping roofs, because it prevents ....
(a) Mountain animals from getting into the house
(b) Flood water from entering into the house
(c) Mosquitoes from entering into the house
(d) Snow from collecting on the roof

22. Match the following Column I with Column II.

Column I	Column II
A. Camel	1. Tallest land animal
B. Cheeth	2. Largest land animal
C. Giraffe	3. Ship of the desert
D. Elephant	4. Fastest land animal

Codes

	A	B	C	D
(a)	1	2	3	4
(b)	3	4	1	2
(c)	4	2	3	1
(d)	2	4	1	3

23. Identify *X* and *Y*.

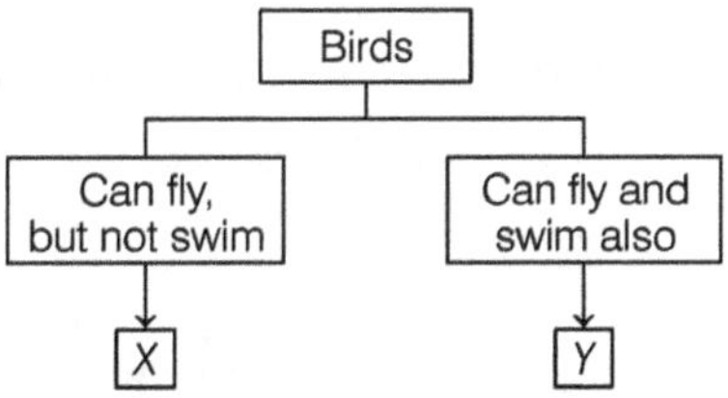

Choose the correct option .
(a) *X* - Sparrow, *Y* - Kiwi (b) *X* - Peacock, *Y* - Duck (c) *X* - Eagle, *Y* - Emu (d) *X* - Duck, *Y* - Kiwi

24. Select the correct statement.
(a) Unlike Moon, stars have their own light.
(b) Unlike stars, Moon has its own light.
(c) Like Moon, stars shine by reflecting Sun's light.
(d) Like stars, Moon appears by twinkling in the night sky.

25. Kartik takes healthy diet daily, still he falls ill frequently. What could be the reason for it?
(a) He does not do his home work daily
(b) He does not trim his nails regularly
(c) He does not wash his hands properly before eating
(d) Both (b) and (c)

26. Select the correct statement.
(a) Paper is made from stem pulp of a tree
(b) Sugar is made from stem juice of grass
(c) Henna is obtained from the leaves of a shurb
(d) All of these

27. Study the give Venn diagram and select the correct option regarding it.

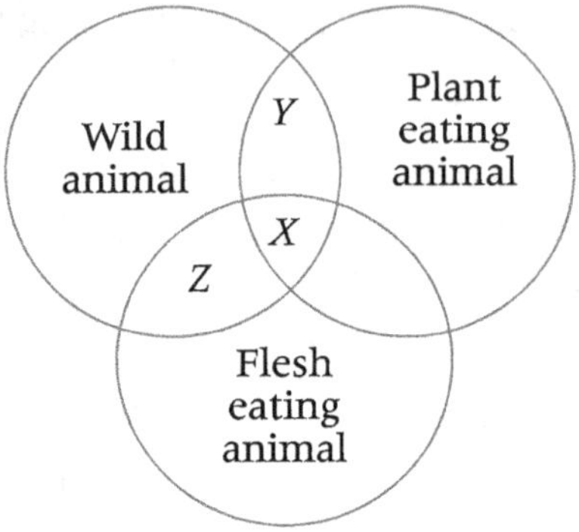

(a) X represents Bear (b) Y represents Zebra (c) Z represents Lion (d) All of these

28. Select the incorrect option.

	Do's	Don'ts
(a)	Drink water after proper purification	Eat uncovered food
(b)	Wash hands before and after meals	Talk while eating
(c)	Eat junk food	Eat food at regular intervals everyday
(d)	Chew food properly	Eat food from roadside vendor

29. Study the given classification chart and select the correct option regarding it.

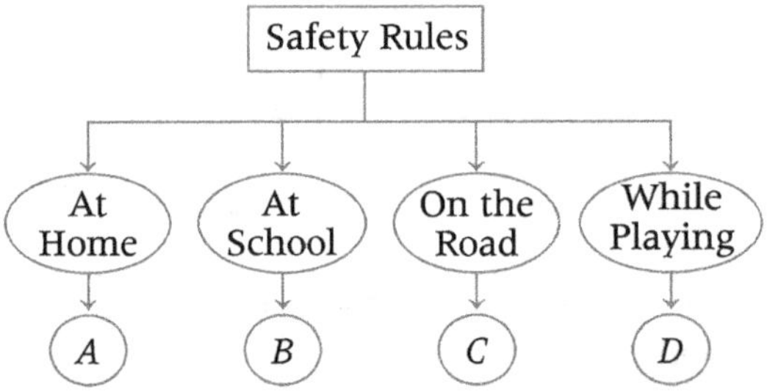

(a) A-Do not touch stoves, heaters, toasters or electric fan when they are switched ON.
(b) B-Do not stand in the queue.
(c) C-Do not fly kites in open fields.
(d) D-Cross the road at the zebra crossing, When the traffic light is green for vehicles.

30.

Sakshi — Moon is closest to Sun

Jaya — Sun is the closest star to Earth.

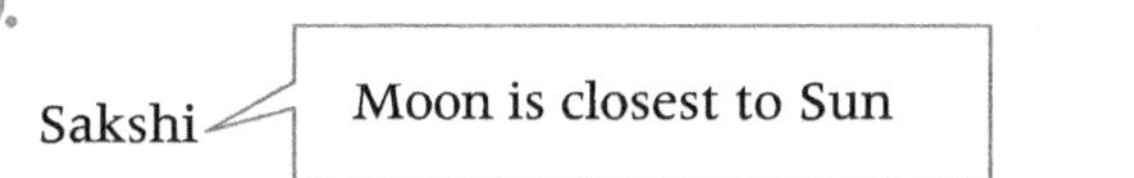

Read the given conversation and select the correct option.

(a) Sakshi is right but Jaya is wrong. (b) Both Sakshi and Jaya are right.
(c) Jaya is right but Sakhi is wrong. (d) Both Sakhi and Jaya are wrong.

31. Study the given flow chart and select the option that correctly fills the empty space *A* and *B*.

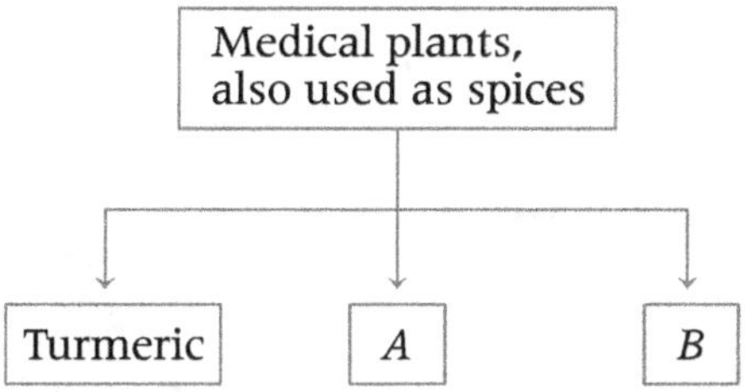

(a) Cinnamon and neem (b) Cardmom and almond
(c) Clove and mustard (d) Tulsi and guava

32. Refer to the given flow chart and select the incorrect option regarding it.

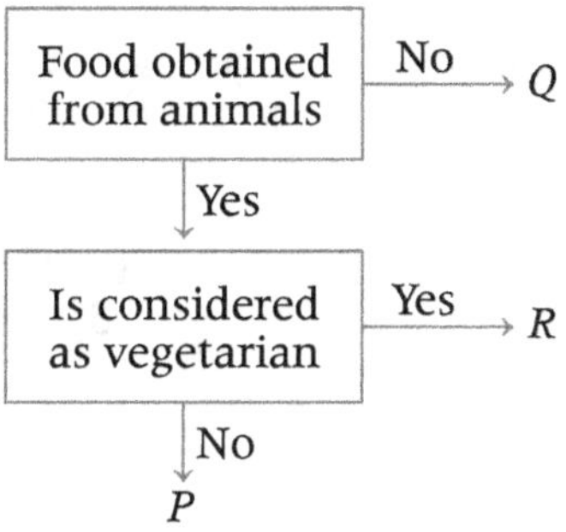

(a) There is no such food item as *R*.
(b) *Q* can be a white coloured energy giving good which is staple food of West Bengal.
(c) *P* can be any of the egg, meat or chicken.
(d) None of the above

33. Which of the following correctly shows the water level when a beaker of water is tilted?

(a) 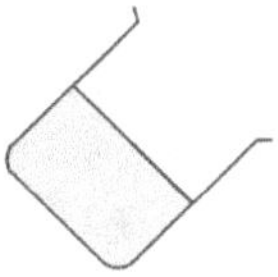 (b) 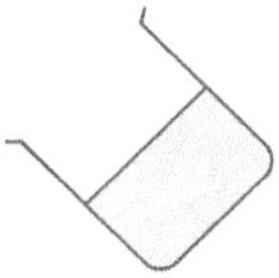 (c) 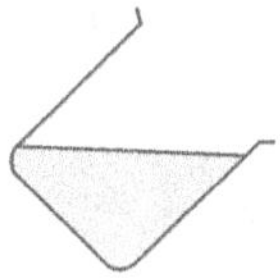 (d) 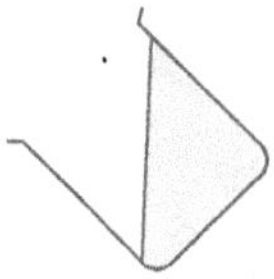

34. Given below is the list of activities that three friends are doing in their classroom.

Yashi — Writing on the walls of the class

Rekha — Running in the classroom

Shanya — Standing on the desk

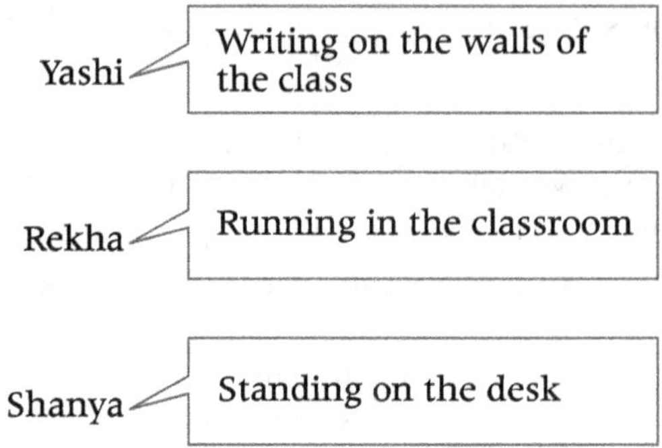

Which child is doing and incorrect activity?

(a) Yashi only
(b) Yashi and Rekha
(c) Rekha and Shanya
(d) Yashi, Rekha and Shanya

35. The cloth shown in the given picture did not absorb water at all, when checked after a few minutes. It is suitable for making a ....

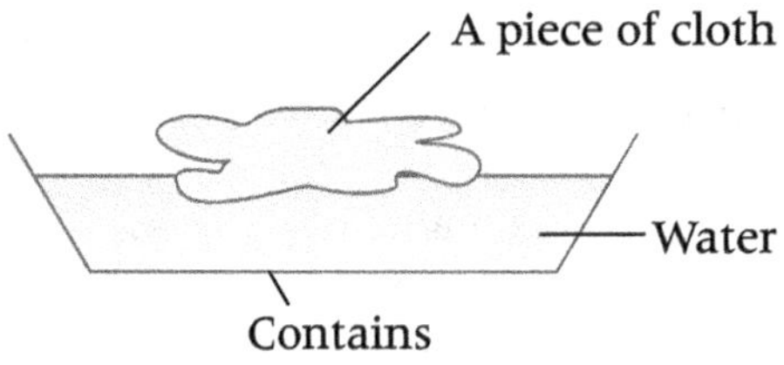

(a) T-shirt
(b) Floor map
(c) Raincoat
(d) None of these

Hints & Solutions

Living and Non-living Things

1. (*a*) There are two kinds of non-living things, natural and man-made.
   The Sun, Moon, clouds, rivers and mountains are natural non-living things. Things that are made by man like chairs, tables, computers, Umbrella, televisions etc., are called man-made non-living thing. Dolphin is a living thing.
2. (*b*) Computer is wrongly placed among living things. It is a man-made non-living thing.
3. (*d*) Plant is a living thing. The Sun, Moon and group of stars are natural non-living things.
4. (*c*) We classified non-living things into two categories namely natural and man-made non-living things.
5. (*c*) Cat, camel and mouse has legs, they all can move from one place to another on their own. But plants do not move from one place to another. They show movement only at their place.
6. (*a*) Both statement I and II are true because plant and dog, both are living thing, so they can grow and move from one place to another and statement III is false, because aeroplane cannot fly on their own as itis a non living thing.
7. (*d*) Sunflower, chick and a baby all are living things. They can grow, become old and then die.
   A brick is a non-living thing. It can not grow, become old and then die.
8. (*b*) All the given characteristics are shown by both plants and birds except option (b). Birds can fly but plants cannot. Plants moves only at their place.
9. (*a*) Bird is a living thing, while aeroplane is non-living thing. Rest differences can be corrected as
   Both can fly. Birds fly on their own, while aeroplane flies with the help of humans.
   Birds can seen in the sky as well as on trees, while aeroplane can seen in the sky as on well as land, but not on trees.
10. (*d*) Animals are living things. They move from one place to another in search of food, water and shelter, they also move to get away from danger.
11. (*d*) Living things have life in them. They need food and water to grow.
12. (*b*) The closing movement of leaves by touching of the touch me not plant tell us that touch me not plant is a living thing and living things can feel and respond.
13. (*a*) Plants make food on their own. Plants need air, water and sunlight to make their food.
14. (*c*) Living things need air to breathe. If living things do not get air, they would die.
15. (*c*) Plants do not have sense organs (*B*), but they can also feel (*A*). Plants grow towards the light. A *Mimosa* plant feels (closes) when touched.
16. (*a*) A seed is a living thing because it grows into a sapling, which grows into a plant and then into a tree.
17. (*c*) Milk is a non-living thing. Tree and men are living things. Cooking oil is a non-living thing. Living things are those which can grow, move, can breathe and reproduce, but non-living things cannot respire, feel, grow and move.
18. (*c*) In option (a) bird is a living thing.
    In option (b) child is a living thing.
    In option (d) trees are living thing.
    In option (c) all are natural non-living things.
19. (*a*) Teddy, chair, car are non-living things that can move by human. Mountain is a natural non-living thing and cannot move by humans.
20. (*b*) Frog needs air to live in the jar because there is no air present in tightly closed jar. Frog needs to breathe. If air is not present in the jar, frog will die after some time.
21. (*a*) All the given options are living things and can move from one place to another except sunflower. Sunflower moves only at their place.
22. (*a*) '*Q*' represents plants. Plants can breathe and grow. They do not have legs, so they do not move from place to place.
    '*R*' represents humans. Humans move from place to place can breathe, grow and have legs.

Plants

1. (*b*) Leaves are known as the kitchen of plant because leaves make food for plants.
2. (*b*) A–Bamboos are used to make furnitures.
B–Tulsi are used to make medicines.
C–Jasmine are used to make perfumes.
D–Sugarcane are used make sugar.
3. (*c*) Plants which are found in desert are called desert plants. *Cactus* is a desert plant.
4. (*b*) Plant 'B' is a pea plant which is climber. They need support to stand straight and grow.
Plant 'A' is grass which is a herb.
Plant 'C' is watermelon plant which is a creeper.
Plant 'D' is sunflower which is a shrub.
5. (*d*) Roots fix the plant firmly in the soil. They absorb water and minerals from the soil for growth of plant.
6. (*c*) The leaves, fruits and seeds of neem tree gives us medicines. It has antibacterial property.
7. (*d*) Mint, coriander and tulsi are herbs. Herbs live for only one season and then die.
8. (*a*) The plant given in picture is cotton plant. Cotton fibres comes from the cotton plants. Jute fibres are obtained from jute plants. Wool comes from sheep and leather is obtained from the skin of animals.
9. (*a*) A–Lotus is a water plant. A water plant is a plant which grow only in the water not on the land.
B–Rose plant is a shrub. These plants are not as big as trees.
C–Mint is a herb. These plants are small with weak stem. They have thin and green stem.
10. (*a*) Wheat is a grass plant. Wheat are used to make chapati and bread. Wheat and rice are food grains which we eat.
11. (*b*) All statements are correct except statement in option (b). It can be corrected as Shrubs are smaller than trees.
12. (*a*) Plants which are used as medicines are called as medicinal plants. Turmeric, tulsi, neem, etc. are medicinal plants.
13. (*a*) Plants which are grown in water are called aquatic plants.
e.g. Lotus, water lily, *Hydrilla*, etc.
Rose and sunflower are not aquatic plant.
14. (*b*) Money plant and grapevine are examples of climbers because they climb up by taking the support of other plants, sticks or walls. Creepers grow along the ground. Herbs are very small plant and shrubs are short and bushy plant.
15. (*a*) We get oil from coconut.
Turmeric is used in food and medicines.
Papaya is used as fruit when ripened and used as vegetable when raw.
Sugarcane is used to make sugar.
16. (*a*) Rose is a shrub plant. Its flowers are used for making perfumes and scents.
17. (*b*) Cotton and jute are examples of fibres. Cotton fibres are used to make clothes, while jute fibres are used to make mats, bags, ropes, etc.
18. (*b*) Rose, cauliflower, lotus and lilly are flowers but cauliflower is an edible flower which is used as vegetable.
19. (*a*) In the given items, there are 6 items which we get from plants, i.e. medicines, cereals, fibres, fruits, vegetables and spices.
We get leather, meat and wool from animals.
20. (*d*) *X*-represents tree. Tree is a big plant. They have strong, woody stem called trunk.
Y-represents shrubs have woody stem.
Z-represents climber. Climbers have weak stem. They need support to stand and grow.
21. (*c*) I. Plant grows from seed.
II. The fruit grows from the flower.
III. Buds grow on the stem.
22. (*a*) Mango, apple and papaya are fruits, which grow on trees except watermelon. Watermelon is a creeper. It grows along the ground.

Animals

1. (*d*) Milk giving animals produces milk. These animals are cow, buffaloes, camel and goat.
2. (*d*) Animals which we are kept in our homes or farms are called domestic animals. They depend on humans for their shelter, food, water and general care.
3. (*d*) Elephant, cow and giraffe are plant eating animals, while tiger is a flesh eating animal.
4. (*a*) A–Rabbit loves to eat carrot.
B–Cat loves to drink milk.
C–Goat loves to eat grass.
D–Elephant loves to eat bushes like sugarcane.

5. (*d*) Honeybees make honey from the nectar of flowers. Butterfly helps in pollination. Silkworm gives silk threads.
6. (*c*) Picture A shows sheeps. These sheeps provide us wool. Picture B shows silkworm. They provide us silk threads.
7. (*d*) Bullock, camels, donkeys, mules, ponies and elephant are used to carry loads. Dogs are used to guard houses and farms.
8. (*a*) A–Cow lives in a shed.
   B–Horse lives in a stable.
   C–Lions lives in a den.
   D–Dog lives in a kennel.
9. (*a*) Oxen are used to plough the field. Horses, donkeys and elephants are used to carrying loads.
10. (*b*) Hen gives us both egg and meat. Duck, ostrich and snake only lay eggs, they do not give meat to us.
11. (*c*) Bear is a wild animal and which eats both plant and flesh of other animals.
12. (*c*) The given animal is camel. It lives in desert and used for carrying loads. It is called as ship of desert. Camel is a herbivore therefore does not feeds on other animals.
13. (*a*) *X*-represent dog. It eats both plants and flesh of other animals.
    Cow and goat are plant eating animals.
    Snake is flesh eating animal.
14. (*b*) Crocodile have four legs and a big-strong tail. It is the one of the strongest animal of water.
15. (*b*) Goat gives us milk as well as meat also, Pig gives meat only.
    Hen gives meat as well as egg also.
    Horse is used to carrying loads for us. It also used for riding.
16. (*c*) The given items are leather items. Leather things are made from the skin of dead animals. We get leather from crocodile, buffalo, snake, etc.
17. (*c*) Snake, tiger, rabbit and rhinoceros are animals which live on land. But fish, whale and dolphin live in water only. Frog lives on both land and water.
18. (*d*) The birds that cannot fly are called flightless birds. Kiwi, penguin, ostrich and emu are flightless birds.
19. (*a*) Butterfly is an insect. It has six legs and colourful wings. It sucks nectar from the flowers.
    Spider is also an insect but do not have wings. Honeybee and mosquito are also an insect but do not have colourful wings.
20. (*b*) Lion is known as king of jungle.
    Tiger is national animal of India.
    Peacock is national bird of India.
    Camel is known as ship of desert.
21. (*d*) Here, *P*-represents lion, Lion lives in forest and eat flesh of other animals.
    Q-represents goat. Goat lives in farms and eat only plants.

Human Body

1. (*d*) There are five sense organs in our body namely Eyes, Ears Nose, Tongue and Skin.
2. (*d*) Our body is made up of bones, muscles and different organs.
   Bones gives shape and support to our body, muscles helps the bones in movement of body, while different organs work to maintain our body's health.
3. (*b*) Stomach helps in digestion of food.
   Lungs helps in breathing. Kidneys help to remove out waste material from the body.
   Heart pumps blood to the whole body.
4. (*c*) Brain is the organ that control all our actions like seeing, hearing, walking and learning. Brain is the controller of whole body.
5. (*c*) Hotness is sense by skin. Eyes and ears used to see things and hear sound respectively.
6. (*a*) Nose helps us to smell (Incense stick).
   Ears help us to hear (Headphone).
   Eyes help us to see (Book).
   Tongue helps us to taste (Cake).
7. (*c*) There are 206 bones in our body. When all bones are arranged in a proper way, they form a skeleton.
8. (*c*) Skin is the largest sense organ in our body. It covers the entire body. Skin helps us to feel things.
9. (*b*) For breathing process, the organ involved is lung not ribs.
   Heart helps in the pumping of blood.
   Stomach helps in the digestion of food.
   Brain helps in the thinking process.
10. (*c*) Skin is involved when Kunal made this prediction. He put his hand in the box and by touching he is able to conclude the nature of the object which is inside the box. Skin helps us in describing whether something is hot, cold, rough or smooth.

11. (*d*) I. We have five sense organs.
II. We see with our eyes.
III. We feel things with our skin.

12. (*b*) Tongue is one of the sense organ. It helps us to taste. It has no bones.

13. (*a*) Stomach is called as store house of food. It helps in digestion of food by storing food for long hours.

14. (*d*) Tongue is our sense organ and helps us to taste. Human tongue can detect different tastes like sour, sweet, bitter, salty, etc.

15. (*c*) The given organ is heart. The main function of heart is to pump blood in the whole body.

16. (*a*) The given organ is brain and it is protected in skull. It controls all of the body system. Our heart is protected by ribcage.

17. (*d*) We have two eyes, two ears, two legs and two hands in our body. Hence, all parts in the given options are paired in our body.

18. (*c*) Option (c) is incorrect statement and corrected as
Skeletal system gives shape and support to our body whereas all other statements are correct.

19. (*d*) The joint is a place where two bones meet. It helps in the movement of bones.

20. (*c*) Cooking food, doing homework and playing badminton are done with the help of hands except watching cartoon it can be done without the use of our hands.

21. (*a*) Eyes help us to see the colour of the cloth, while our skin help us to know the cloth is soft by touching it.

22. (*d*) Given organ is kidney. It is bean-shaped organ. It helps us to remove waste material from our body.

23. (*b*) *P*. represents nose. It helps us to smell and also helps in breathing.
Q. represents lungs. It helps in only breathing.

24. (*a*) Sonu can differentiate a cup of hot tea and a mug of cold coffee by touching them.
She cannot differentiate a piece of red and blue cloth because she was blindfolded, she cannot see the colours of cloth.

25. (*d*) The given structure of bones is called ribcage. The ribcage protects the heart and the lungs.

Food and Nutrition

1. (*c*) Most of the food, which we eat comes from plants and animals. Plants are the major source of food for human beings and other animals. Animals provide us food materials such as milk, eggs, chicken, meat, fish, etc.

2. (*a*) Plants gives us fruits and vegetables. Several spices, pulses and herbs are also obtained from plants. Animals gives us meat, egg, milk, etc.

3. (*c*) We get carbohydrates from rice, potato, wheat and fats from butter, ghee, etc. Carbohydrates and fats give us energy.

4. (*c*) Fruits and vegetables and provide us vitamins and minerals. They protect us from illness. That's why they are called as protective food. They keep our eyes, skin and gums healthy.

5. (*d*) We need food to live and grow. Food provides us energy to work and play and to remain healthy.

6. (*d*) The body building foods (proteins) like milk, eggs, chicken, fish, etc., help us to build our muscles and body to grow, while bread and rice are energy giving food and fruits are called protective food.

7. (*d*) Pizza, burger and chocolates are junk food. Fruit such as apple is a healthy food.

8. (*d*) Apple, papaya and pomegranate are fruits. They are called as protective food. All fruits are rich in vitamins, minerals, carbohydrates, etc. hence, they are protective food.

9. (*a*) Neha should eat rice and chapaties to get energy. These food items are rich in carbohydrate.

10. (*d*) Eggs are not fatty food. They have proteins. They are body building food. They help in the growth of the body. They also help in the repairing of injured parts.

11. (*b*) People who eat fish, meat and chicken are called non-vegetarian, while people who do not eat fish, meat and chicken are called vegetarian. They only eat vegetables and fruits.

12. (*a*) Mummy says us to eat green vegetables like spinach because they are protective foods. Green leafy vegetables protect us from bacteria, viruses and other infections.

13. (*b*) A–Milk is rich in calcium.
B–Dal and roti is rich in carbohydrate.
C–Eggs are rich in protein.
D–Cold drinks are junk food.

14. (*d*) Tomato soup is made from tomatoes. Bread is made from flour. Thus, tomato soup, bread and chick peas are obtained from plants. Omelette, chicken and milk are obtained from animals.

15. (*c*) Cucumber can be eaten raw. It is eaten as salad. Rest all the food items can be eaten only after cooking.

16. (*c*) Balanced diet contains only healthy food with proper amount. It contains all three kinds of food namely protective, energy giving and body building food.

17. (*c*) Correct statements are
I. Wash fruits and vegetables before eating.
II. Cereals are plants products. They are obtained from plants.
III. All vegetables should not be taken as raw, they should be cooked before eating.

18. (*b*) Orange is not a fat rich food. It is rich in vitamin-C. Rest all foods are correctly placed.

19. (*b*) Fruits and vegetables are protective food. Sugar or sweets are energy giving food. Chicken and meat are body building food.

20. (*b*) If raw food items are cooked, then there protective nutrients may be lost due to heat. Eating raw food is also tastier and full of nutrients.

21. (*c*) Milk is called a complete food because it helps us to grow make our body strong, it protects us from falling sick and it gives us energy to work and play. It is a body building food. It is also a protective food and it is also energy giving food. It is the only food given to a newborn baby.

22. (*d*) *P* represents egg. It is the richest source of protein for non-vegetarian as it comes from animal source. *Q* represents soybean. It is the richest source of protein for vegetarian person.

Housing and Clothing

1. (*b*) A hut, tent house and caravan are temporary house and these houses are not strong. A house made up of bricks, cement and steel is a strong house.

2. (*c*) Eskimos who live in very cold, snow bound regions make igloos from snow to live in. These igloos are warm from inside and protect the eskimos from cold.
While kutcha house is made up of mud and clay. Pucca house is made up of cement, bricks and iron.

3. (*a*) A tent house is made up of canvas. It can be folded and carried along easily. Campers, nomads, soldiers and construction workers use this type of house.

4. (*c*) House provide us protection from heat, cold, storms, wild animals, etc.

5. (*b*) Sweaters, shawls, woolen gloves of winter cap are use to protect us from winters.

6. (*a*) People who live in igloos are called eskimos.
Gypsies live in caravans.
Campers live in tents and wild animals live in forest.

7. (*a*) A - Sweater and gloves are used in winters.
B - Short pants are used in summers.
C - Raincoats and gumboots are used in rainy seasons.

8. (*c*) We wear thin cotton clothes on hot days as they keep our body cool.

9. (*b*) Kutcha house is made up of mud, straw, stones, bamboo, etc.
Cement is used in making pucca house.

10. (*a*) Cement is used to make the walls of building. Wood, rubber and plastic are not used to make the walls of buildings.

11. (*a*) Houseboats are mainly found in Kashmir and Kerala. These houseboats are commonly known as Shikara.

12. (*c*) Our house contains bedrooms, kitchen, hall, bathroom, etc. while playground is present outside the houses.

13. (*b*) The corrected form of statements are
I. Kutcha houses are not strong only pucca houses are strong.
II. A hut is made up of materials like grass, mud, bamboo, straw, etc.

14. (*d*) Sweaters, gloves and socks are made from wool, while sarees are made from silk, chiffon, etc.

15. (*a*) A tent house is not a permanent house. The picture (a) show a tent house made up of bamboo. It is a type of traditional tent used in some regions.

16. (*b*) Cotton, silk and wool are natural fibres. Cotton is obtained from cotton plant.
Silk is obtained from silkworm. Wool is obtained from hairs of sheep.
But rayon and nylon are synthetic fibre.

17. (*c*) A. Mobile house – Caravan
B. Floating house – Houseboat
C. Dome-shaped house – Igloo

18. (*c*) Fibres that are made by humans are called man-made fibres. Nylon, polyester, rayon and acrylic are examples of man-made fibre.

19. (*c*) The incorrect statement is (c), because only kutcha house is made up of mud, grass, bamboo, etc.

20. (*b*) A–Cotton is the fabric that keeps us cool in summer.
B–Wool is the hair of animals which is used to make clothes.
C–Waterproof materials does not let water to pass through.

21. (*d*) The picture shows the winter season. In this season, we wear sweaters, gloves, etc., to keep ourselves warm. Cold, dry air blows in this season. In this season, we light fire to keep us warm.

22. (*d*) The given picture is of a stilts house. These houses are raised from the ground level on bamboo stilts. These houses are made in areas, where it rains heavily. This does not let the water or snakes enter the house.

23. (*d*) It is a picture of a building. They have many homes, each of them is called a flat. These houses are very strong and are made from bricks, cement and steel.

24. (*a*) We called caravan as house on wheels. This house is also known as mobile house.

Safety and First Aid

1. (*d*) We should follow safety rules anywhere and everywhere we go. Following safety rules, makes us safe from getting hurt.

2. (*c*) A skull and crossbones is a common symbol used as a warning of danger, particularly in regard to poisonous and dangerous things.

3. (*d*) Avoid touching pointed or sharp edged objects like needles, knifes, blades, etc. These objects may cut your skin or body parts that will hurt you and lead to injury.

4. (*d*) The following safety rule one must follow while travelling in a bus
   - Stand in a queue, while waiting for or boarding the bus.
   - Stay seated while the bus is moving.
   - Talk softly to the bus driver, so that he can concentrate on driving.
   - Do not lean out of a moving bus.

5. (*a*) Pedestrian crossing is also known as zebra crossing. It is the black and white strips on the roads we should always cross the road at the zebra crossing.

6. (*b*) I. We should not swing on windows. This can cause accidents.
II. We should not play on road. For playing, parks are made.
III. Hold hands of parents on roads.
IV. Obey traffic lights.

7. (*d*) While riding a bicycle on the road, one should always keep to the left of the roadside to stay safe and alert.

8. (*c*) In figure A, people are using footbridges to cross the road. This is a safety measure for crossing the road.
In figure B, boy is walking on the footpath. One should always use footpath, while walking on road.
In figure C, people are crossing the road at the zebra crossing.
In figure D, children are getting into the bus in a queue.

9. (*a*) The immediate help given to an injured person is called first aid. Always keep first aid box with yourself.

10. (*c*) Do not touch electric wires, switches, electric gadget and plugs with wet hands. You might get an electric shock.

11. (*a*) Never talk to strangers and do not accept sweets or chocolates from them.

12. (*c*) The main aim of giving first aid is to save lives and keeps the person comfortable till medical help arrives.
First aid is the first help which is given to the injured person.

13. (*c*) We should not rush down the staircase otherwise we may fall and can get injury.

14. (*b*) A box that contains things like cotton, antiseptic lotion and band-aid needed to give first-aid to an injured person is called a first-aid box.

15. (*c*) We should not talk on the mobile, while driving. It may cause accident on roads.

16. (*d*) We can play with ball and badminton in playground. Screwdriver, scissors and knife are sharp objects. We should not play with sharp objects.

17. (*c*) If the dog bites you firstly wash the wound with soap and water and after that apply antiseptic lotion. Rest matches are correct.

18. (*c*) Figure (a) shows that we should not quarrel/fight with our friends during swinging and wait for turn.
Figure (b) shows that we should not take any part of your body out of the vehicle.
Figure (c) correctly shows children walking on the footpath or on the safe side of the road.
Figure (d) shows that we should not stand on the furniture in the classroom.

19. (*b*) We should always fly kites in open grounds not on the terrace or on the road. Flying kites on the terrace is dangerous as chances of slipping or falling down may occur.

20. (*a*) Only E comb your hair daily is wrongly placed in don'ts list. It is a good habit and safe, so should be placed in do list.

21. (*b*) When the pedestrian light is red, it indicates that the pedestrian must not cross the road. It says 'Stop'. When pedestrian light is green, it says that people can cross the road. When pedestrian light is yellow, people should wait.

Air, Water and Weather

1. (*b*) Moving air is called wind. Wind can help us in many ways. Wind moves a sail boat. Wind turns the blades of a windmill.

2. (*c*) Rain fills up the rivers, lakes, ponds and wells. This water is then used by human beings and animals. Sea water is not fit for drinking, as it is salty.

3. (*b*) There are five seasons in India namely summer, rainy, autumn, winter and spring.

4. (*a*) A–gentle wind is called breeze.
B–Air contains water in the form of water vapour.
C–We should breathe clean air to stay healthy.
D–Hottest season is summer.

5. (*c*) Air cannot be seen. It only feels when it moves. Air is colourless, odourless and tasteless.

6. (*a*) Boiled water is better than normal water because boiling kills microbes. Boiled water is good for health. It reduces the chances of infection.

7. (*c*) Rainy season comes in July and August. We saw rainbows after rains.

8. (*d*) Freezing is not the correct method to kill the germs in water. Boiling is a method which is used to kill the germs. We should always boil water before drinking. Other matches are correct.

9. (*b*) Dust and smoke makes the air polluted. The dust, smoke and germs originate from the factories and vehicles. These things causes air pollution.

10. (*a*) Winter comes in November to January. It is the coldest season.

11. (*b*) A - Gumboots are made up of rubber and used in rainy season.
B - Air has weight.
C - Windmill produce electricity with the help of wind.
D - Solid form of water is ice.

12. (*d*) We should breathe in clean air to stay healthy. Things that can be done to keep the air clean are
- Do not burn wood.
- Plant a tree.
- Walk or use a bicycle instead of other vehicles.

13. (*a*) '*X*' represents rain. Rain falls from clouds and fill ocean, river, etc.

14. (*a*) In autumn season, trees shed their leaves. This season comes in September and October.

15. (*c*) The incorrect statement is
Air contains dust and smoke only.
The correct form of the statement is
Air is a mixture of gases such as oxygen, nitrogen water vapour, smoke, dust and germs.

16. (*c*) The correct statements are,
I. Drinking water should be stored in clean vessels.
II. Containers with drinking water should be covered.
III. It is only our duty to save every drop of water.

17. (*c*) An umbrella is used in both summer and rainy season. In summer, it protects from direct sunshine and in rainy season, it saves us from getting wet.

18. (*b*) Air takes up space. When we blow air into a balloon, it fills the space inside the balloon. Air filled in a football and tyres takes up the space inside and gives them their shape.

19. (*a*) In spring season plants put new leaves and flowers bloom everywhere. It is the most pleasant season.

20. (*c*) Anu's statement is correct about air. Sonal's statement is wrong as air has no taste. Air is present all around us. It does not have colour, taste and feeling, Air is required by all the living organisms.

21. (*a*) When ice get heated, it melts and water is formed. This water when get heated, it turns into water vapour.
Similarly, when water vapour gets cooled, it gives water and when this water get cooled it forms ice.
water is present in three forms which can be changed.
22. (*c*) The experiment shows that air is needed for burning. This is because the candle had used up all the oxygen in the glass and when all oxygen is used up, it is not able to burn anymore and get extinguished.
23. (*d*) When rain falls on ground, some water absorbed by plants, while some water goes deep down in ground. Rainwater fills oceans lakes, rivers, etc.
24. (*a*) The weather forecast predicts heavy rains on Monday, moderate rains on Tuesday, partly clouds on Wednesday. Cloudy on Thursday and partly cloudy again on Friday. It indicates that the prevalent weather is rainy and it is a monsoon season. Suman will use raincoat, umbrella and gumboots to protect herself from rain.

Our Surroundings

1. (*a*) In figure (a), a traffic inspector is instructing the public about the traffic.
In figure (b), a police inspector is there.
In figure (c), a soldier is there.
In figure (d), a lawyer is there.
2. (*d*) Tailor is a person who stitches uniform, dresses, etc.
3. (*a*) The given picture shows a joint family consisting grandparents, parents and their childrens.
4. (*a*) Barber is a person who cuts hair and style them. They also known as hair dresser. Barber helps him to get a new haircut.
5. (*d*) Milkman gives milk and newspaper hawker delivers newspapers. They both comes to our house everyday, early in the morning.
6. (*b*) Chemist is a person who sell first aid materials and medicines prescribed by doctor. Sarita should go to a chemist.
7. (*d*) A nuclear family consist only mother, father and their children. Grand parents and other relatives are not a part of nuclear family.
8. (*a*) Watchman is a person who guard our houses, colonies, etc. watchman will take care of the safety of our house in our absence.
9. (*a*) Your uncle's son is related to you as cousin, while nephew is your brother's or sister's son. Niece is your brother's or sister's daughter.
Uncle is your father's or mother's brother.
10. (*d*) Given tools are used by carpenter for making furnitures.
11. (*b*) For build a house, plumber, architecture, engineer, electrician, carpenter, etc. will helps. Barber is not required to build a house.
12. (*a*) On a front of an ambulance van, there is a + sign. It is called a sign of emergency.
13. (*b*) Railway station is the place where trains regularly stop to load or unload passengers.
14. (*b*) Hospital is a place where you will see doctors, patients, nurses, etc.
15. (*a*) Tailor does not need comb to do his work. Comb is needed by barber.
16. (*a*) In the given figure, man has a letter in his hand. He is a postman. Postman brings letter and parcels for us.
17. (*a*) A person does a job to earn money.
A person doing any kind of job is known as its occupation.
18. (*d*) (A) Kalpana Chawala was an astronaut.
(B) M. S. Dhoni is a cricketer.
(C) Narendra Modi is our prime minister.
(D) Abdul Kalam was a scientist.
19. (*b*) Teacher teaches in schools and colleges.
20. (*a*) Policeman maintains law and order in cities.
21. (*d*) Soldier is in the army who wears uniform and has gun.
22. (*a*) Farmer grows crops, fruits and vegetables.
23. (*b*) Doctor treats patients.
24. (*c*) According to Rahul's statement. He is not feeling well thus, he should visit a doctor. Ritu needs to buy a new crayon set, so she should visit a stationer.
25. (*a*) Mrs. Rubi teaches you Maths, she is a teacher. Mr. Ramesh bakes cake for you, he is a baker.

Our Universe

1. (*a*) Our solar system has 8 planets namely, Mercury, Venus, Earth, Mars, Jupiter, Saturn, Uranus and Neptune.
2. (*c*) The planet *B* in the solar system is Saturn. This planet has rings and due to the presence of rings it is unique and called as ringed planet.

3. (*d*) Stars cannot be count. They are uncountable.
4. (*b*) Earth is also known as 'Blue planet' because of presence of water. About three-fourth of its surface is water and one-fourth is land.
5. (*b*) We see tiny stars at night. Stars has its own light in the sky.
6. (*a*) Jupiter is the largest planet in our solar system and Saturn is the second largest planet.
7. (*d*) Mercury, Venus, Earth, Mars, Jupiter, Saturn, Uranus and Neptune are eight planets of our solar system.
   The Moon is a natural satellite of the Earth.
8. (*b*) Moon is the natural satellite of the Earth. It moves around the Earth only.
9. (*d*) Option (d) is incorrectly matched.
   The correct matches are
   (a) Evening star - Venus
   (b) Red planet - Mars
   (c) Coldest planet - Neptune
   (d) Smallest planet - Mercury
10. (*c*) The Sun is a big ball of burning gases which gives out both heat and light.
11. (*c*) The Sun is our nearest star. It is a huge ball of burning gases that gives us light and heat. It is the head of the solar system.
12. (*a*) Sun looks like a big ball of fire. It gives us heat and light.
13. (*c*) In our solar system, Earth is placed at IIIrd position. Ist is Mercury, IInd is Venus and IVth is Mars.
14. (*b*) The Sun rises in the East and sets in the West.
15. (*d*) We can see that the shadows are longest during the morning and evening and shortest during the afternoon.
16. (*c*) Statement in option (c) is incorrect and can be corrected as. All stars (including Sun) have spherical shape.
17. (*b*) People, who visit the space are called astronauts. The astronauts are those who go to the Moon wear special space suits that protect them from the harmful rays of the Sun.
18. (*c*) All statements are true except statement in option (*c*) because Sun is a star not a planet.
19. (*a*) The Moon changes its shape day by day. The Sun, stars and all planet never change its shape.
20. (*d*) Planets do not have a light of their own. They reflect the Sunlight that falls on them. This make planets glow.
21. (*c*) Moon is smaller than the Sun and the Earth. The Sun is bigger than the Earth. So, the increasing order is
    The Moon < The Earth < The Sun.
22. (*b*) *P* represents star. Star neither moves around the Sun nor is the part of our solar system. Star has its own light.
    Q represents Moon. Moon neither moves around the Sun nor it have its own light. Moon is the part of our solar system.

Practice Set 1

1. (*b*) Food items like milk, fish, meat, eggs, pulses, green peas, chicken help us to grow. They make our bones and muscles strong. These food items are called body-building food. Protective food protect us from infection. Energy giving food gives us energy for the good functioning of body.
2. (*c*) Coconut tree is a big plant, rose plant is a shrub and mint is a herb plant.
   So, the increasing order according to their size is Mint < Rose < Coconut
3. (*c*) A–Wood of some plants such as bamboo and pine is used to make paper.
   B–Flowers of rose plant are used to make soaps, shampoos and perfumes.
   C–We get jaggery and sugar from sugarcane.
4. (*b*) The correct statements are
   It is not safe to play or run on the road.
   When the traffic signal shows red, the vehicles should stop.
   It is necessary to obey all the traffic rules because road accidents happen when people do not follow the traffic rules.
5. (*c*) A gentle wind is called breeze. Leaves of a tree rustle when a breeze blows.
   A strong wind is called a gale.
   A very strong and noisy wind is called a storm.
6. (*c*) Cotton plant yields fibre.
   Barley yields maize.
   Tea plants yield tea leaves.
   Mustard plants yield mustard oil.
7. (*c*) The person in the given figure is a diver. Diver dives inside the water. He explores the world of the sea.

8. (*c*) Seeds are mostly contained in the fruits. Different fruits contain different types and number of seeds.

9. (*c*) Water changes from one form to another when it is heated or cooled. Ice, water and water vapour or steam are the three different forms of water.

10. (*c*) Picture-A is of a tree.
Picture-B is of a herb.
Picture-C is of a creeper.
Picture-D is of a shrub.

11. (*d*) Swimming in the pond will not pollute water. Washing clothes in the pond, animal bath and washing motor vehicles will lead to water pollution.

12. (*b*) Carrot is a modified root, not a modified stem. Modified root stored food in them.

13. (*a*) We get a sticky juice from a tree named acacia, which is used to make gum.

14. (*d*) A–Gorilla lives in open places.
B–Snake lives in a hole.
C–Tiger lives in a den.
D–Bear lives in a cave.

15. (*b*) Clothes dry quickly on sunny day and windy day. Rainy day does not allow the clothes to dry due to higher water content of air.

16. (*c*) We have five sense organs: eyes, ears, nose, tongue and skin.
Brain is the thinking organ of our body. It is not a sense organ.

17. (*d*) Head is the body part, which has all the sense organs present in it. There are five sense organs which help us to see, smell, touch, taste and hear. They are skin, nose, mouth, ears and eyes.

18. (*b*) A–Goat gives us milk.
B–Hen gives us eggs.
C–Bees gives us bee wax to make candle.
D–Sheep gives us wool.
Which is used to make sweater.

19. (*c*) Posture is the position of our body while sitting, standing or walking. A good posture keeps us healthy and in good shape. It is neither a soft part our body nor a hard part of the body. It is also not the framework of bones.

20. (*c*) I. The Sun gives us heat and **light**.
II. The half of the Earth that faces the Sun has **day**.
III. We have day and night because the **Earth** rotates.
IV. Moon shines due to the light of the **Sun**.

21. (*b*) Animals like deer, elephant, rhinoceros, giraffe, monkey and zebra eat only leaves, grass, green plants and fruits. These animals are called plant eating animals. Animals like tiger, bear, lion eat only flesh of other animals. These animals are called flesh eating animals.

22. (*c*) We wear light cotton clothes on hot days as they keep our body cool.
We wear thick woollen clothes in winters as they keep our body warm. Raincoat is used during rainy season.

23. (*d*) The experiment shows that air has weight. When two balloons are placed on the rular they are equal. But, when one balloon gets pricked. The rular moves upward on the side where the balloon was deflated.

24. (*d*) We can keep the air fresh and clean by walking or using a bicycle instead of other vehicles that produce smoke and by planting trees.

25. (*a*) We should not play with electricty. Playing with electricity can cause electric shock. We should not play with fire.
Washing the floor is a good habit.

26. (*c*) The main function of lungs is to take oxygen and give out carbon dioxide and the process is known as breathing.

27. (*c*) Stilts are houses, which people build with sloping roofs in the areas where it rains heavily so that the rainwater can easily fall from the roofs.

28. (*a*) Good food habits help us to stay healthy and protect us from falling sick.
Good food habits are wash your hands with soap before and after eating every meal.
Eat freshly cooked food. Eat your food at regular interval.

29. (*b*) A house floating on a lake is called house boat. A houseboat is a boat that has been designed or modified to be used primarily as a home.

30. (*a*) Eight planets move around the Sun. The path in which planets revolve around the Sun is called orbit. The planets are Mercury, Venus, Earth, Mars, Jupiter, Saturn, Uranus and Neptune.

31. (*b*) The smallest bone of our body is present in ear. The stapes is the smallest bone in the human body which is present in our ear and Femur is known as the longest bone of human body, it is present in thigh.
32. (*b*) We should drink freshwater to remain healthy. Fresh water is generally characterised by having low concentrations of dissolved salts and other total dissolved solids.
33. (*b*) The process of photosynthesis is carried out by leaves. Photosynthesis, the process by which green plants make their food in the presence of Sunlight. Photosynthesis is also known as the food making process of plants.
34. (*c*) If Ankur is suffering from cough and cold, then he must have to visit the doctor, because cough and cold are type of infection so, if he visit to the doctor, then doctor would prescribe him some medicine which make him fit again.
35. (*b*) Most of the living organism's need oxygen to breathe. Most of the living organisms inhale oxygen. Mainly human beings and animal require oxygen for breathing and oxygen that we inhale is comes from the plants and trees.

Practice Set 2

1. (*a*) Flowers are responsible for producing fruits in a plant. If all the flowers are removed from a plant, then it will not produce fruits.
2. (*d*) We should never play with matchbox and blade. It may hurt you.
3. (*a*) Mercury is the smallest planet of our solar system.
4. (*c*) Eating too many chocolates and sweets is harmful for our teeth and it can cause cavities in the teeth.
5. (*c*) *X*-represents orange, Orange plants has all the parts.
   Y-represents rose, Rose has all the parts but do not have fruits.
6. (*d*) Raj is married to Vaishnavi hence Vaishnavi is wife of Raj.
7. (*b*) Rahul should give signals before taking turns.
8. (*a*) Neptune is the outermost planet of our solar system and is thus, farthest from the Sun.
9. (*c*) Egg, fish and chicken are body building food, while bread is an energy giving food.
10. (*b*) We use our eyes to see different things like the shining raindrops on leaves.
11. (*d*) We should not follow the following habbits, they can harm animals that is, overloading the load carrying animals, throwing stones at animal and tying fire crackers on the tail of stray animals.
12. (*c*) Sugar and cocoa are plant products and honey is an animal product. Salt is obtained from sea water.
13. (*d*) Somya should do the first aid and call elder, so all the given option are incorrect.
14. (*b*) Water vapour is a gaseous state of water while rain and dew are liquid states of water and snow is the solid state of water.
15. (*a*) Balanced diet is a diet that contains all the nutrients in right amount. For a balance diet, we must take some food from each group in every meal. Butter oil should be consumed in least amount as excess of these food items can be harmful for our health.
16. (*b*) Men is wrongly placed under Non-living things as men come under living things.
17. (*b*) It is a cotton plant. It is a shurb as it is a small bushy plant and has hard stem and branches.
18. (*a*) Lungs are the breathing organs. The air we take in through nose reaches our lungs. If a person has difficulty in breathing, it means that has some problem in his lungs.
19. (*b*) Varun most probably be residing in a place where floods are common and heavy rainfall occurs.
20. (*a*) We should eat proper quantity of food at a time. Stuffing the mouth with food can lead to choking.
21. (*d*) Snow slides off the sloping roofs, hence does not collect on it.
22. (*b*) Camel is ship of the desert, cheeth is fastest land animal, giraffe is tallest land animal and elephant is largest land animal.
23. (*b*) Peacock, sparrow and eagle are birds that can fly but not swim.
    Duck is a bird that can fly and swim also.
    Emu and kiwi, both are flightless bird.
    Here '*X*' represent peacock and '*Y*' represent duck.
24. (*a*) Moon is a natural satellite that revolves around the Earth. It does not produce its own light, instead shines by reflecting light falling on it from the Sun. Stars, on the other hand, are huge balls of fire and produce their own light.

25. (*d*) Dirt and germs collect in long nails and enter our mouth with food that we eat.
Dirty hands also carry germs. These germs when enter ourbody, causes diseases. This is why kartik falls ill, frequently despite of taking healthy diet.

26. (*d*) Paper is obtained from stem and pulp of trees.
Heena is obtained from leaves of a shrub.
Sugar is obtained from sugarcane.

27. (*d*) Bear is a wild animal that eats both flesh and plants. Zebra is a wild animal that eats plants only. Lion is a wild animal that eats flesh only.

28. (*c*) We should not eat junk food because it is unhealthy and overeating of junk food may result in diseases like obesity. We should eat food at regular intervals everyday, as it helps in proper digestion of food.

29. (*a*) A-'At home', do not touch stoves, heaters, toasters or electric fan when they are switched ON. They could be dangerous While other option incorrect.

30. (*c*) Jaya gives the correct statement that is sun is the closest star to Earth and Sakshi give wrong statement because mercury is nearest planet to the Sun.

31. (*c*) Clove and mustard have medicinal properties and they are also used as species.

32. (*a*) Milk, butter, cheese etc are considered as vegetarian food items because their production does not involve killing of animals.

33. (*c*) In beaker (c) the water level is correct because when we tilted the beaker in right direction, the water also goes with direction.

34. (*d*) We should not write on the walls of the class, its is a bad habbit. We should also not stand on the desk or run in the classroom as we can fall down and get hurt.

35. (*c*) The piece of cloth was kept in the container having water for few minutes. It did not absorb water at all. It shows that the piece of cloth is waterproof and is suitable for making raincoat.

www.ingramcontent.com/pod-product-compliance
Lightning Source LLC
Chambersburg PA
CBHW080004180726
48002CB00020B/3086
* 9 7 8 9 3 2 5 5 1 9 3 1 2 *